Dark Chaucer: An Assortment

DARK CHAUCER

AN ASSORTMENT

Edited by

Myra Seaman, Eileen Joy,
and Nicola Masciandaro

punctum books ✳ brooklyn, ny

First published in 2012 by
punctum books
Brooklyn, New York
http://punctumbooks.com

ISBN-13: 978-0615701073
ISBN-10: 0615701078

Library of Congress Cataloging Data is available from the
Library of Congress.

Cover Image: detail of a photo of Le Parc Régional
d'Armorique, western Brittany, France, chosen for its
allusion to the 'grisly rokkes blake' along the coastline
that plague and worry Dorigen in Chaucer's *Franklin's
Tale.*

Facing-page drawing by Heather Masciandaro.

for Lee Patterson

 PREFATORY NOTE

> . . . there is no escape from history into romance.
> ~Lee Patterson, *Chaucer and the Subject of History*

> . . . *stultus in tenebras ambulat* [the fool walks in darkness]
> ~Ecclesiastes 2:14

> . . . by the shadwe he took his wit
> ~Chaucer, *The Man of Law's Tale*

This little book had its genesis over a dinner shared with friends — Nicola Masciandaro, Öykü Tekten, Karl Steel, and Eileen Joy — in a restaurant in Brooklyn on April Fool's Day in 2011, the same day that saw the launch of punctum books. As we were sharing some food and wine and joking around about this and that, Nicola mentioned that he had always wanted to write a book or edit a collection of essays that would focus on all of the dark and melancholic places in Chaucer (of which there are many, once you start paying attention), and while teaching Chaucer over the years, he has been collecting these dark moments in his head and ruminating them like small black pearls. This also recalled to Nicola how frequently Lee Patterson uses the term "dark" in his book *Chaucer and the Subject of History*. Chaucer is, of course, widely beloved for his playfulness and comic sensibility, but his poetry is also rife with scenes and events and passing, brief instances where everything could possibly go horribly wrong or where every-thing that matters seems, if even momentarily, altogether and irretrievably lost. And then sometimes, things really do go wrong.

It struck us that evening that in order to do justice to these moments, which are more numerous than you realize when you start looking for them, that you would have to be willing to fall into these abyssal passages without ropes and without worrying how everything ultimately turns out (this would be a rogue journey against the teleological tides of the narratives and over the beachheads of certain comforting scholarly "resolutions"). The idea would be to undertake something like soundings in the darker recesses of the Chaucerian lakes and to bring back palm- or bite-sized pieces (black jewels) of bitter Chaucer that could be shared with others — an "assortment," if you will. It could be productive (and hell, interesting), we thought, to gather together some shipmates who would be willing to explore Chaucer's darker topographies, and even get lost there, not so much making sense of these dark passages, or referring them to how things ultimately turn out, but rather, making them more rich and more strange, like the pearls that were in Alonso's eyes as he sank to the bottom of Shakespeare's ocean in *The Tempest*. Myra Seaman stepped in to help steer; others were impressed into service.

Opting to dilate rather than cordon off this darkness, this volume assembles a variety of attempts to follow such moments into their folds of blackness and horror, to chart their endless sorrows and recursive gloom . . . as if there were no way (back) out. Not that this collection finds only emptiness and non-meaning there. You never know what you will discover in the dark.

Eileen A. Joy and Nicola Masciandaro
Cincinnati, Ohio | Brooklyn, New York

TABLE OF CONTENTS

☺ and here we are as on a darkling plain

Gary J. Shipley

§ (BARRINGTON) THE OLD MAN IS DARK IN LIGHT AND

blackening, like a corpse-reanimate, lost in nights of stars of heaven's sick white light. And there are hilts wired to the widening grip of bleached palms, the edges remaining white beneath a spill of blood carved black. And each love and loveless seed of rot is white, leeching lignin and degrading and decolorizing all past worlds of woods of tar-black trees rooted in some foreign shame. And though the fox of this wood is black and the cabbages white in which it lays, there is no peroxide in the throat that trolls the art of stories of old things.

§ (BRYANT & ALIA) THERE BEFORE HILARITY AND LOVE, DARK STRATAGEMS

eating (fetal earth and rock from under towers), entombing navvies in the rubble of inestimable black skies — like poor Arcita crushed inside the shadow of his horse. Out from the obscurity of their cells that discordant love, itself as all love born of mutilation, reigns an exalted illness of human meat. Saturnian remembrances of gold oiled with broken necks, and saturate lungs with poison-strangled hearts, and quod bodies rotting into walls, of leonine interment with tongues black with disease and eyes and men blotted by duplicity, by genocidal plagues and buried breathing: the succoured whims of justice from a father's hundred hands.

§ (EVANS) THE SOGGY FLESH OF DREAMS

tears like the crepe of sleep between the fingers of the sun, waking half-alive to the feel of mourning crepe that still eludes her untouched arm. The sea fills him in a way that sleep cannot, making cold dark shipwrecks of his organs and hard blind barnacles of his eyes. For though the worm of sleep ingeminates the husband's airless cadaver, no solution may be concocted with his wife. When he speaks his words are sounded senseless black inside black ears, in a language made of wounds made shed of bodies that cannot wake, so that all the wife can see before she dies are water lines of shadows drowning in icy silences of noise.

§ (GILBERT) THE DISLOCATION SHEDS FALSE LIGHT

into tarnished muscle transported vertically outside a wink. And so for all sick faces of this fair the book is the only mask prescribed, empyreal eyes the only glue. The devil up and like his tongue spreads outwards, squirming shapeless through endless bodies of the dead and living made again for earthly torment. That summoner dragged to Hell to know a true fiend's measure… But enough now of gallows fruit and war, and instead a modish sun dripping through them vaulted cracks. And to conclude, all ends are porous bones, skeletons sucked clean and dipped in fire, each scrap of marrow absorbed and lit eternally by the raging firestorms of some long-spurious glow.

§ (HARRISON) OF THESE MANY KINDS OF MURDER

this poet's see-through suicide is one. The knife goes in without a sound, so old and harrowed is the flesh it turns. Behind the words, then, an evacuee, from some sweaty industry of bloodless tongues. And with no alterity to fill the gap, the wounds are left to pile, up with little notion of return like rotten cityscapes bloated black and windowless with some unspent and poisoned coin. This voiceless livestock, once made of caves and unwalled hearts, will soon grow fat enough to eat, and the factory they made of human life will consume them whole and over inside the noise of war.

§ (MASCIANDARO) A DAY FOR EACH BUNGLED STROKE

her body and her head remain, annexed by the yawning neck of some adamantine law. A bath of fire leaves her skin untouched; and three desperate slashes, of one annihilator's knife, fail to carve the martyr from the meat. Her lungs in this half-lived hinterland, inflated with a mesial air, find veins in stasis congruent, a doomed division having left them half-measured with her blood. St. Cecilia in her semi-death, a torture made by God and shadows into nothing, lives this way aborted by her theomorphic spine, until the hour when emptied of the earth they bear her cold concluded corpse to it.

§ (MITCHELL) FROM THE SLICK SALIVA OF THE SEA

black mangling rocks protrude like diabolic teeth. The Franklin, with an eye forever in his stomach, makes her distant husband into food. The devil's jagged mouth has no reason to exist. And should she find a reason, it too could just as readily dissolve. Maybe the rigidities that terrorized could flow again in blood, dripping off the handle of the dagger in her chest. She and the tale might flow again, the lithic impasse having been repulsed for good, by the silent horror of a graveyard stone. Tension grows like sediment, congealing, the tale poising to prorogue, until alteration remains unchanged and what was rock begins to move.

§ (NEEL & RICHMOND) IT SPREAD ITS WINGS IN BLOOD

across Arcita's face: a bird of ill portent gesturing toward man's inevitable black flight. Once white it sang of love's betrayal, of a man-shaped insect that crawled inside a wife, and was seen by him betrayed to be tainted by the song, and so with an arrow in his spouse he turned his fury on the bird.

This crow's demise, from pure unpigmented songbird to muted blot of smut, is itself the omen, both well and ill, of all that love can be. To the devil scorched and mumchance: the bleak and vicious course of failing in the game constructed from the lustre that it maims.

§ (PRIEST) THE GRIEF EXACTED BY ABSENT MEN —

the impalements, the drownings, the lovers and the children strung up by the neck — is, in Custance, itself embroidered in absentia. The sea is at its kindest when corroding, like rain at night, and her eyes once lacrimal are rusted shut to wake. Unused she drifts and shipwrecks, her mind as her virtue bleached as white as teeth, with no red stain of massacre conjectured by the snake. Her face so often bloodless barely masks its void, and any promised colour as vain and flimsy as the Arab satin that scooped her out and set her on her way, some crude vessel rudderless and lost.

§ (SCHAMESS) THE THING'S FAILURE TO ERASE ITSELF

is detailed in a florid gore, in scars and burns — eroticized in spastic horror and vicarious omnipotence — and jerk responses to its pain. The gall will colonize its bodies and rule them mostly from within. (It infiltrates at places felt but never seen, and fucks its victim in the arse to perpetrate its dream.) Each kneeling orifice is the fantasmatic embodiment of an other, and all intestines left, nothing but raw and weeping cankers on some obscene coagulate of jelly. With this tension like a palimpsest's surface script forever scraped away, the cohabitation veers towards a sinless carcass, rigid and insensible.

§ (SEAMAN) LIFE ABDUCTED AND PRESERVED,

in headless, burnt or flooded animation, does not belie the trauma that it was, but serves instead to reaffirm the grip of its myopia. Like the Fairy King's mutilated horde, some limbless some insane, we live fortified in drowsiness and in gold, and yet suspended ask again for further deadening. A corpse with the merest purpose has more art and life than those that though still living stand enervated by the air they breathe. In suffering, as in death, man is torn small; and makes his art (a narcotic catch basin) from the pieces that remain, his eyes averted from the crudity of origins or the aqueous dissolution of their fate.

§ (STEEL) DREAMS OF KINDNESS, LUST OR JUSTICE, EITHER ONE,

can and do inseminate the wombs of death and life and purity. And they poison with external purpose that which, untainted and autonomous, was coded in ambivalence toward anything but its own elusion. Like this they're made solutions to the quandaries that have locked them in: whether stuck in the sand of a life that will not otherwise recede to sea, or finding one's identity preserved in that which ends it, or else as fair prize in a skirmish to the death. Each one of these three saintly women is made pinion of a story; stories, each of which, remorseless and determined to rot her from the outside in.

§ (TREHARNE) THE VESTAL'S HEAD, HAVING MOURNED ITSELF, IMPLORED

to be removed from the site of its proposed corruption. That way in her father's hand, suspended by her hair, she'd never be unmade, maculate and breathing. The fanatic vigilance, preached by the physician and found reflexive in the virgin, looks out to put the law inside – yet still too readily is she dirtied from without. Her headless corpse, its heart once warm now tepid and disabled, is the fate of this unyielding celibate, whose passion to preserve was the match of any to defile, but alas the pull of death's the same for martyr as for rogue. If the sinful must always find their due — disembowelled, their blackened insides out — then the sinless, to remain it seems, must find their equal spilled in white.

§ (Valasek) Even well-intentioned schemers

must squirrel sickness in the dark: his gift for rhetoric and murky stratagems finds sport in others, in the very claustrophobia of desire. Manipulative and seeking wings, he'll orchestrate the union, or else, like Cupid clipped, forever feel the weight of not. Our intrigant though detached is not omniscient, so cannot see the latent doom his instrument must face, nor the instrument that he too has become. His ignominious defeat is floodlit, and the limits of his ingenuity shown built from incalculable human matter. And so with all attendant eyes impaired with light, nobody sees the puppet nurse its contaminated heart, left to beat now until its end in a thousand or more dimmed pieces.

§ (Weston) When you make your God from fear,

from all the paths you cannot choose between alone, you make your praying mouth a trauma and its every dribbled word a tomb. God's adherents see their love reflected just as clearly in the gleaming knife, as it passes through a throat, as in the still fresh waters gifted benignly from the sky. In zombiism as in zealotry, there's no response to send us quailing on the earth. For the songs we sing in innocence will echo regardless of the substance of the walls, and the evil bodies, pissing doubt and excrement, will once dismembered make a veil.

§ (White) The skeleton, its bones tied up in rhyme,

is yanked in ceremony from the meat it braced to become instead a frame. The architect of this once romantic structure is hushed and ridiculed inside the work and out, and like his doggerel obscured by shit you could not buy. And the desecrated tissues left behind prolong themselves through melting, hiding in the shade of those custodians that rape. But still within this black beyond there is gravity to witness: a malformed colossus skewered with a lance, each of its three

heads remade in agony, with screams that echoed out and on
forever — down into man's nerves further than any ear.

Dark Whiteness

Benjamin Brawley and Chaucer[1]

Candace Barrington

On the northern edge of the Boston Commons, at the intersection of its Freedom Trail and its Black Heritage Trail, stands a life-sized relief commemorating Colonel Robert Gould Shaw. While tour buses pause at the adjacent red light, microphoned guides repeat what walkers can read from the posted information: the white Colonel Shaw led the all-African-American Massachusetts 54th Regiment, the first of its kind, into the Civil War. Among the hundreds of thousands of men who served and died in the American Civil War, Shaw is singled out, not because he fought and not because he died, but because he granted military legitimacy to the brigade of African-American troops who were otherwise not allowed to fight in their own cause. Augustus Saint-Gauden's monumental bronze centers Colonel Shaw on horseback, with his regiment members preceding and following. Although these men walking with the hero were cast with facial features identifying them as African-American, their skin color is indistinguishable from the military leader's because his is darkened to the same hue by the bronze. In effect, Saint-Gaudens' memorial does what no war and no legislation has been able to do: erase the color difference, not by making all the men white but by making all the men dark.

[1] My deepest thanks to Audrey Kerr, Valerie Allen, Erick Kelemen, Myra Seaman, and Michael Shea for their thoughtful comments on this essay.

I open with this racial-blurring vignette because Benjamin Brawley (1882–1939), an African-American scholar, educator, and poet who eulogized Shaw in verse, also eulogized Chaucer in verse.[2] Like Saint-Gauden's memorial, Brawley's poem "Chaucer" darkens its hero while praising Chaucer's transformative role in English literary history. The poem reminds us that while the category of race is invisible in *The Canterbury Tales*, it has left in Chaucer's reception a series of indelible marks that can be difficult to discern. This essay attempts to see through the centuries of assumed whiteness to the moment when Brawley darkens Chaucer's reception. To see this transformation, I will first examine the faces both in Chaucer's tales and of his readers, before providing a series of three readings of Brawley's "Chaucer." In do so, I will show how Brawley's poem goes beyond celebrating Chaucer to establish the African-American versifier as a legitimate successor to the Middle English poet, thereby staking a claim for African-American poets as the source of the next innovation in English letters.

§ WHITE CHAUCER

White faces fill Chaucer's *Canterbury Tales*. Their ubiquity can be easy to ignore because they are not labeled as white. Aside from the occasional lady with the fair face — which could refer to her skin tone, her beauty, or both — skin color is noteworthy in Chaucer's tales not as a visible, essential

---

[2] In using the terms "race" and "white" and making distinctions based on skin color, I am using terms and making distinctions with wide currency and credibility when Brawley wrote at the turn of the twentieth century. Though those terms and distinctions remain in use in popular culture, their credibility in the academy had been undermined well before the end of the century. For a succinct analysis of the shift, see Karim Murji, "Race," in *New Keywords: A Revised Vocabulary of Culture and Society*, eds. Tony Bennett, Lawrence Grossberg, and Meaghan Morris (Malden: Blackwell, 2005), 290–296. So while Brawley argued against racial discrimination, he did not argue against the existence of racial distinctions.

bodily quality but as a changeable trait linked to such external factors as climate, work, and habit. The ruddy faces of churls and imbibers show the results of their labors and their leisures. The faces of the distraught turn pale with worry or death. And the skins of Perkyn Revelour ("brown and as berye" [I.4368]) and the canon's yeoman (with a "leden hewe" [VIII.827–88])[3] manifest the visible consequences of meddling in the nefarious affairs of London's back streets. None of the exotic Saracens or Asians populating *The Man of Law's Tale* or *The Squire's Tale* are noted for their dark-hued skin. The closest a foreign character comes to being dark-skinned is Emetreus, "the king of Inde" whose facial "colour was sangwyn / A fewe frakenes in his face yspreynd / Bitwixen yelow and somdel blak ymeynd" (I.2156, 2168–2170). The one reference to a dark-skinned Ethiopian is lodged within a simile describing the way the desert heat had transformed St. Jerome's skin while leaving his lechery intact (X.345). And if we scratch that simile a bit, we find the Ethiope's dark skin is not an essential attribute, for just below its surface is the Biblical notion that overexposure to the southern sun produced the sable-skinned Africans. No matter how exotic the characters or how foreign their origins, Chaucer's *Canterbury Tales* show us no naturally dark-skinned man, woman, or child. Dark or ruddy skin in Chaucer's work is a consequence of sin, sun, damnation, or putrefying flames; it is not a natural condition for the *Tales'* characters. Whether describing knight or peasant, merchant or pirate, ruler or saint, man or woman, Englishman or Saracen, Chaucer seems to have assumed his characters were white-skinned until tainted by some corrupting influence. So as we imagine his kaleidoscope of characters, some exemplary in their perfection and most identifiable in their humanity, we must imagine a world that begins, by default, unrelentingly but invisibly white.

---

[3] All references to Chaucer's *Canterbury Tales* works from *The Riverside Chaucer*, gen. ed. Larry Benson, 3rd edn. (Boston: Houghton Mifflin, 1987), by fragment and line number.

That essential whiteness would seem to extend to writers who have found inspiration in Chaucer's tales: Gower, Hoccleve, Lydgate, Spenser, Shakespeare, Milton, Dryden, Wordsworth, Browning, Eliot, and Woolf, a litany of dead white males sprinkled with the names of a few white women. This reception history records their friendly, even filial, affection for the poet credited with creating a space for English vernacular verse. Even as they remake Chaucer's works, they comment on the short distance they feel between themselves and the medieval poet. In joining the loud chorus of readers who find in Chaucer what they are or hope to become, they contribute to the Chaucerian whiteness.

This persistent whiteness of Chaucer's reconstruction permeates the darker moments in his reception history. During England's imperial expansion into territories inhabited by darker races, Chaucer was carried along in the form of inexpensive duodecimos and middlebrow anthologies as a marker of British cultural superiority. Closely identified with British hegemony, Chaucer was an integral part of the colonists' attempts to assert Anglo-Saxon excellence and to maintain close connections to the British homeland. There is no evidence that the colonized held Chaucer in similar esteem or affection. Neither his name nor his works were appropriated by the non-white, indigenous peoples as a vehicle for their own concerns, as, say, Shakespeare has been. And in the United States, where colonization was influenced by the diasporas of slavery and immigration, Chaucer inspired pens more often held in white than in black hands.

And yet Chaucer's tales would seem ripe for appropriation in ways not pursued by African-American authors. For example, the *Canterbury Tales*, with its collection of tale-telling travelers from diverse estates and professions, would seem to be an attractive source text for transposing those social categories into ones more influenced by race and ethnicity. Yet, as far as I can tell, no African-American author has made such an appropriation. In addition, until the middle of the twentieth century, the African-American dialect was considered a juvenile form of Modern English, comparable from twentieth-century Americans' vantage to Chaucer's equally immature Middle English, which John Dryden admired as "a rough Diamond" that "must be polish'd e'er he shines."[4] As Ellery Sedgwick — the long-time editor of *The Atlantic Magazine* and dean of American high culture — relates when he pauses in his memoir to note the compositional style of an African-American housekeeper, her writing is unshackled by either the niceties of spelling or the rules of grammar, "artless and vivid like that of some happy pilgrim of Dan Chaucer."[5] Though Sedgwick records this observation after dialect verse had lost any currency, it illustrates the primitive affinities the white literati saw between Chaucer's Middle English and African-American dialect, making it an attractive source text for appropriation into dialect poetry, a wide and easy path to success for African-American writers in late nineteenth-century America. Despite this linguistic affinity, no one has made use of it. Finally, although Chaucer's bawdy humor and multi-syllabic rhymes makes his verse an ancient predecessor to late-twentieth-century hip-hop, there's been no darkening of Chaucer here, either. Baba Brinkman, the major redactor of the *Tales* into rap, keeps the pilgrims and their tales within an all-white world. Perhaps this whiteness darkens momentarily with Jay-Z's "99 Problems"; these 1990s lyrics about African-American urban culture include the line "If you don't like my lyrics you can press fast forward," a distant echo of Chaucer's admonition that those readers offended by the Miller's churlish tale should "turn the leef over and chese another tale" (I.3177). Except for this tantalizing bit, neither hip-hop nor any other predictable places reveal a darkened Chaucer.

To find an African-American poet appropriating Chaucer's name and verse we must to turn not to the places of obvious affinity, but to an area where Chaucer stands as the

---

[4] John Dryden, "Preface," *Fables, Ancient and Modern*, in *The Works of John Dryden*, vol. 11 (London: William Miller, 1808), 229.
[5] Ellery Sedgwick, *The Happy Profession* (Boston: Little, Brown and Son, 1946), 211–212.

father of English verse, an agent of white cultural dominance. Here we find Benjamin Brawley's poem from the turn of the twentieth century, a short moment in American letters when African-American authors sought to abandon their racial blackness, to molt and become white by adopting the values and skills prized by the dominant classes. In his scholarly works and in his pedagogy, Brawley advocated that African-American students, intellectuals, and poets should adopt mainstream values of thought and speech to demonstrate their intelligence, education, and equality to the white learned classes.[6] He believed the arts would be the place where the African-American genius would rise to its greatest distinction, but in order to be recognized as such, African-American art would have to be made in accordance with the standards promoted by the white elite.[7] For Brawley, this first meant being steeped in the Anglo-Saxon literary heritage. He read and admired Britain's canonical authors — Chaucer, Shakespeare, Milton, and Wordsworth — and their respected expositors at American universities, such as Kittredge at Harvard and Manly at the University of Chicago. For these reasons, he disdained the sentimental and supplicatory dialect poetry associated with Paul Laurence Dunbar, and he criticized the vernacular and raw literature associated with the Harlem Renaissance.[8] These values shape the sonnet he published in 1908 entitled "Chaucer":

> Gone are the sensuous stars, and manifold,
> Clear sunbeams burst upon the front of night;
> Ten thousand swords of azure and of gold
> Give darkness to the dark and welcome light;
> Across the night of ages strike the gleams,

---

[6] Allen Flint, "Black Response to Colonel Shaw," *Phylon* 45.3 (1984): 210–219.

[7] Benjamin Brawley, "The Negro Genius," *The Southern Workman* 44 (1915): 307–308.

[8] John W. Parker, "Benjamin Brawley and the American Cultural Tradition," *Phylon* 16.2 (1955): 183–194.

And leading on the gilded host appears
An old man writing in a book of dreams,
And telling tales of lovers for the years;
Still Troilus hears a voice that whispers, Stay;
In Nature's garden what a mad rout sings!
Let's hear these motley pilgrims wile [sic] away
The tedious hours with stories of old things;
Or might some shining eagle claim
These lowly numbers for the House of Fame![9]

For over a century, the poem has been dismissed because its glorification of Chaucer seems too complicit in the continued whiteness of the English literary canon.

It's easy to see why readers have long assumed the poem is at best a race-neutral work praising the genius of Chaucer, and at worst a capitulation to white hegemony, the oppressive master.[10] To see how it contributed to this reputation, one does not have to look very deep. To begin, "Chaucer" joins the hoards of conventional, turn-of-the-century verse praising this or that hero or noteworthy event. By writing in this commonplace genre, Brawley signals his efforts to join the literary mainstream. Additionally, the poem situates its praise by associating Chaucer with the bright light of daybreak, which has invaded the nighttime with "[t]en thousand swords of azure and of gold." This association is further refined in the second quatrain, where the conflict between light and dark is redefined as the conquest of the benighted past's darkness by a "gilded host" led by an "old man writing." This enlightened author is identified as Chaucer by allusions to his corpus: his early dream poetry, *Troilus and Criseyde,* and the *Canterbury Tales.* Chaucer, according to these lines, is the author responsible for driving away the darkness and bringing the

[9] Benjamin Brawley, "Chaucer," in James Weldon Johnson, ed., *The Book of American Negro Poetry,* rev. edn. (New York: Harcourt, Brace, 1958), 151; hereafter referred to by line numbers.
[10] John W. Parker, "Toward an Appraisal of Benjamin Brawley's Poetry," *CLA Journal* 6 (1962): 55–56.

light of a new literary age. In this accepted reading, "Chaucer" is an over-the-top praise of the Father of English letters, and it is easy to assume that Brawley is holding up Chaucer as his literary hero to be emulated but never matched, a form of white love.

§ BLACK CHAUCER

However, not far beneath this laudatory reading of the poem lies a second, one which begins to darken Chaucer's reception in two ways: it incorporates Brawley's lyric speaker into Chaucer's Canterbury-pilgrim audience, and it transforms Brawley into Chaucer's apprentice, an African-American poet able to adopt the master's techniques. We are alerted to this darkened reception by Brawley's shift in syntax towards the end of his allusions to Chaucer's verse. This shift, marked by "Let's" (11), moves the speaker and his audience into *The Canterbury Tales'* embedded audience, the storytelling "motley pilgrims" (11), thereby expanding Chaucer's social categories to include one structured around darkness and whiteness. Moreover, in joining his contemporaneous audience with the *Tale's* medieval pilgrims, Brawley, by extension, affiliates his lyrical voice with that of the master storyteller, Chaucer, whose whiteness brings prestige and literary opportunities to his dark-skinned disciple. The young poet's confident gesture is magnified by what appears to signal his humility: identifying his verse as "lowly numbers" (14). In the context of Chaucer's *oeuvre*, however, Brawley isn't overcome by modesty. Instead, he is making a Chaucerian move, akin to bidding his "litel book" to "kis the steppes" of "Virgile, Ovide, Omer, Lucan, and Stace" (*Troilus and Criseyde* V.1789–92) and joining the company of canonical authors. He demonstrates his worth by publishing the poem (with its meticulous use of the sonnet form and standard English diction) in a solidly white forum, *The Harvard Monthly.* In this second reading, Brawley has taken the first step toward darkening Chaucer's reception by embedding himself in the poem as both auditor and apprentice.

In echoing Chaucer's gestures toward establishing his work as a literary classic, Brawley makes his own claim about setting a new form of English vernacular poetry alongside the traditional canon. To understand what that new form of English vernacular verse would look like, we need to return to Brawley's broader ambitions. Throughout his career, Brawley sought to demonstrate how black artists could absorb white culture and then surpass it by mining the rich and complex African-American experience. We can see these broader ambitions in his long-term scholarship recovering African-American history and letters from obscurity. Beginning with *The Negro in Literature and Art* (1910), and continuing with *A Short History of the American Negro* (1919) and *A Social History of the American Negro* (1921), Brawley sought to write the story of African-Americans and preserve their literature. He understood that whoever controlled the literary texts, no matter how well they measured up to canonical standards, controlled how they were remembered — or if they were remembered at all. Rather than allow the standard Anglo-centric historical and literary narratives to erase African people's presence in America, he seized control of the story and urged African-American poets to add their voices to the register of literary greatness. With this in mind, we can begin to understand how "Chaucer" goes beyond praising or emulating Chaucer's literary values and, in a third level of reading, gives those values a dark face. In this way, the poem reveals that Brawley's ambitions — for himself and for African-American poets — were much grander than his readers generally suppose: the African-American poet is the next logical step in the evolution of English verse inaugurated by Chaucer.

In this third reading, images of darkness and light work together to demonstrate that the white verse of Chaucer and his descendants will be improved by the African-American verse inaugurated by Brawley and a new generation of African-American authors. As the first two readings note, Chaucer's emergence is represented by daybreak, an image invoking the classical tradition of the Apollonian sun as the source of poetic inspiration. The image of light displacing the darkness, however, is less stable than it first appears because the initial source of light — "sensuous stars" — can be read as representing light or, because stars are a synecdoche of nighttime, as darkness. Although this image teeters between light and darkness, the reader is not given an opportunity to consider the choice because the stars are "gone" before they are introduced, and soon thereafter "clear sunbeams" of light conquer the dim lights of the night with "ten thousand swords of azure and gold." The sun's light — which both inspires poets and darkens skins — dominates.

The conspicuously indeterminate fourth line — "Give darkness to the dark and welcome light" — suggests, however, that the light should not be equated with a white, Eurocentric culture. Here, "dark" and "welcome" are syntactically ambiguous, while "darkness" remains a stable noun, no matter how we construe "dark" and "welcome." What changes is the metaphorical tenor of "darkness," which does depend on how we understand "dark" and "welcome. " On the one hand, "welcome" can be a verb parallel to "give," thereby making "dark" a noun. Read this way, the sunrise's golden swords welcome the light, and "darkness" becomes a metaphor for erasure, making the sunrise eliminate the dark of night. On the other hand, "welcome" can be an adjective parallel to "dark," and the welcome light is also a dark light.[11] In this case, darkness doesn't erase or eliminate the light; rather, it intensifies a quality the "dark and welcome" light already has. In this reading, the exotic swords cast their darkness upon the light, not remaking it into their image but bringing out the qualities of the dark and exotic inherent in the light. Reading "welcome" as an adjective gives the first quatrain's imagery a kind of paradoxical circularity: stars, nighttime's lanterns, are dispelled by the brighter light of the

---

[11] For a different reading of this line, see Jay Ruud, "Declaiming Chaucer to a Field of Cows: Three Twentieth-Century Glimpses of the Poet," *Proceedings of the Tenth Annual Northern Plains Conference on Earlier British Literature* (2002): 9 [8–21].

sunrise's exotic beams, which in turn transform daylight by intensifying its inherent darkness. Thus, when we reach the closing couplet, which asks us to see a syntactical parallel between "some . . . eagle claim" (13) and the earlier "Let's hear" (11), the lyric voice and his audience can choose either to listen to Chaucer the master poet or to witness these new poetic lines, lines that dare to darken the white literary tradition, set on the altar at the House of Fame (14).

Thus, while paying homage to the father of English verse and making claims to his part in the English literary tradition, "Chaucer" also repeatedly asserts that the dark will transform the white light. Brawley achieves this not by transforming Chaucer's characters or imagining dark-skinned readers. Instead, he darkens the light that represents the innovation introduced by Chaucer. This is a subtle gesture that, at first reading, deflects attention away from the appropriator. But as my readings show, those rays coming from the dark and exotic margins are the source of the innovation. This innovation is a process that can be appropriated by anyone who approaches the light from the darkened margins. It is infinitely repeatable. Therefore, "Chaucer" is not hero worship — or white love — but the realization that one aspect of Chaucer's art is within reach. And it doesn't matter that Brawley provided no new tradition himself; what matters is that he imagined that the tradition — and its innovation — can appear in darkened tones and be propelled forward to new achievements.

Saturn's Darkness

Brantley L. Bryant & Eight Anonymous Contributors

If we're thinking of a dark Chaucer, Saturn's speech in the *Knight's Tale* comes quickly to mind (I.2453–2478).[1] Although pop culture misguidedly loves *The Canterbury Tales* best for its fart jokes, the appearance of the old, pale god in the first of the pilgrim stories shows that Chaucer can get very dark indeed. Saturn's darkness, this essay will argue, should remind scholars of Chaucer to be attentive to our own ineradicable darknesses. We should see our moments of collapse and chaos not just as unfortunate circumstances to be acknowledged (though that is needed desperately) but also as "ways in" to the most vital and distinctive aspects of our discipline.[2]

---

[1] All references to Chaucer's *Canterbury Tales* are to *The Riverside Chaucer*, gen. ed. Larry Benson, 3rd. edn. (Boston: Houghton Mifflin, 1987), by fragment and line number.

[2] Many thanks to Eileen Joy and Nicola Masciandaro for early suggestions about the direction of this essay, to Susan Nakley for crucial bibliographic suggestions and for thoughts on a very early draft, and to Myra Seaman for invaluable editorial input. Deep and heartfelt thanks go to the eight contributors who were courageous enough to let their words become part of this essay. A core inspiration for this piece is the discussion in Aranye Fradenburg's *Sacrifice Your Love: Psychoanalysis, Historicism, Chaucer* (Minneapolis: Minnesota University Press, 2002), especially 1–78, 239–252. I write in solidarity with Margaret Price's essay "It Shouldn't Be So Hard," *Inside Higher Ed*, February 7, 2011: http://www.inside highered.com/advice/2011/02/07/margaret_price_on_the_search

I want this piece to explore our shared experience in the profession, so, in writing it, I sought the contributions of scholars of medieval literature who have dealt in one way or another with anxiety and depression (clinically diagnosed or otherwise), those unwelcome interventions of Saturn. Eight anonymous contributors sent in lengthy discussions of their experiences, and shared thoughts on the ways that the Saturn of the *Knight's Tale* might help us think about feelings that are very often unwelcome or unacknowledged in academia. The contributors' responses have shaped this essay and its readings of *The Knight's Tale*, though the larger conclusions remain my own. Although the limited scope and methods of this study mean that it cannot make sociological claims or pretend to statistical significance, I hope that readers will keep

---

_process_for_those_with_mental_disabilities. Out of the immense amount of *Knight's Tale* criticism, I draw on the following for this essay: David Aers, *Chaucer, Langland, and the Creative Imagination* (London: Routledge and Kegan Paul, 1980), 174–195; Peter Brown and Andrew Butcher, *The Age of Saturn: Literature and History in the* Canterbury Tales (Oxford: Blackwell, 1991), 1–19, 205–250; Alan T. Gaylord, "The Role of Saturn in the 'Knight's Tale,'" *The Chaucer Review* 8.3 (1974): 171–190; Robert W. Hanning, "'The Struggle Between Noble Designs and Chaos': The Literary Tradition of Chaucer's *Knight's Tale*," *Literary Review* 23.4 (1980): 519–541; V. A. Kolve, *Chaucer and the Imagery of Narrative* (Stanford: Stanford University Press, 1984), 85–157; H. Marshall Leicester, Jr., *The Disenchanted Self: Representing the Subject in the* Canterbury Tales (Berkeley: University of California Press, 1990), 295–321; A.J. Minnis, *Chaucer and Pagan Antiquity* (Cambridge: D. S. Brewer, 1982), 108–143; Lee Patterson, *Chaucer and the Subject of History* (Madison: Wisconsin UP, 1991), 165–230; Gillian Rudd, *Greenery: Ecocritical Readings of Late Medieval English Literature* (Manchester: Manchester University Press, 2007), 48–67; David Wallace, *Chaucerian Polity: Absolutist Lineages and Associational Forms in England and Italy* (Stanford: Stanford University Press, 1997), 104–124. For Saturn lore, I rely on Raymond Klinbansky, Erwin Panofsky, and Fritz Saxl, *Saturn and Melancholy: Studies in the History of Natural Philosophy, Religion, and Art* (New York: Basic Books, 1964).

in mind that the thoughts shared here could very likely be those of their teachers, colleagues, students, and friends.

Now let's think more about that dark speech, in which we learn that a disastrous god is in control of the *Knight's Tale*. A Lovecraftian figure of cosmic misfortune who lurks at the outskirts of the universe, Saturn uses his speech to proclaim his mastery of violent death, disorder, disease, and collapse (I.2453–2478). He rules over literal darkness (the prison in the "derke cote") and over the symbolic darkness of secrecy and betrayal, the "derke tresons" he claims as his own.[3] The chilling images of Saturn's speech also evoke a "darker" view of life, a world filled only with meaningless suffering and sudden political unrest, presided over by the uncaring forces that topple buildings and engender the Black Death's apocalyptic destruction. Saturn's role in the tale's plot, and his speech, are entirely original additions not found in the *Knight's Tale*'s Boccaccian source; Saturn demands our attention because he is a quintessentially Chaucerian invention.[4]

Duke Theseus struggles against this formidable darkness. After Saturn engineers Arcite's death, Theseus responds with lavish ceremony, political stagecraft, and public speaking in an effort to mitigate the sorrow of the young man's death and offer an image of order to contrast with Saturn's uncaring chaos.[5] Astrological lore holds that Saturn's malignant

---

[3] The words I use here appear frequently in scholarship on *The Knight's Tale*. The word "darkness" is ubiquitous. For example, Gaylord, 171; Kolve, 123; Leicester, 367; Patterson, 207. "Malevolent" is also frequently applied to Saturn (for example, Gaylord, 175; Minnis, 139; Patterson, 203). Another common Saturnine word is "chaos."

[4] See Aers, 179–180; Butcher and Brown, 213–224; Gaylord, 176; Hanning, 533–534; Kolve, 125–126; and Leicester, 318–319.

[5] As Patterson notes, Charles Muscatine established a tradition of seeing "order and disorder as the central theme of the tale," which continues with variation in much of the criticism (165); see also Kolve, 125. Patterson claims that both Theseus and the knight seek closure in a way that exposes their failure to find it (200–230).

influence can be counteracted by the power of Jupiter, the
deity whom Theseus imitates; fittingly, Theseus tries to light
up the darkness Saturn creates in the tale.[6] But Theseus's light
is costly, restrictive, forced. In preparing the funeral ceremony
for Arcite, Theseus lays waste to the natural world.[7] In his last
attempt at correction and consolation, the "Firste Moevere"
speech, the Duke fails as well. The lengthy oration presents
little more than a compelled faith in a Jovian order from
which Theseus himself benefits, a glorification of chivalric
fame that the tale's own narrative leads us to distrust, and a
concluding disavowal of the world as a "foule prison" whose
end result is a world view scarcely brighter than Saturn's but
much more constricting in its vision of drearily repetitive
succession (I.3060).[8]

The distinction the tale makes between Theseus and
Saturn, I propose, gives us a way of reading our own work
together as scholars. Too often, I would argue, despite our
best intentions, we are Thesian in our approach to our
profession; we create a show of well-tailored display at great

---

Theseus's "personal control over all aspects of statecraft" is noted by
Wallace (117). Fradenburg notes the tale's contrast between Theseus
and Saturn, observing that one source of "puzzlement" in the tale is
"the perplexing relation between Saturn's arrangements and
Theseus's final speech" (*Sacrifice Your Love*, 166).

[6] Gaylord, 183.

[7] An observation made by Rudd, who treats Theseus's destruction of
the grove at length (58–63). See also Kolve, 131.

[8] This negative view of Theseus is fundamentally inspired by Wallace
(104–124), and draws heavily from Butcher and Brown, especially
their claims that Theseus's argument is based on "faith" in Jupiter's
"repressive" rule, and that it is Theseus's enterprises that have most
clearly caused "the ruination of existence" (235–236). "Better the
vaunted injustices of Saturn," Butcher and Brown write, "who does
encourage dissension and revolt" (236). Aers also provides a crucial
anti-Thesian reading. Theseus's concluding speech is critiqued (for
its failure, its ironic effect, or its lack of coherence) by Aers (188–
194), Leicester (364–365), and Patterson (203–205). Kolve claims
that the speech "ends in a metaphor of despair" and "shows reason
confounded, not triumphant" (148).

cost, and we suppress the very Saturnine darknesses of our lives, either in order to boast about our self-sufficient scholarly virtues or to promote a "business as usual" acceptance of the "foule prison" of structural injustices in our profession and our institutions.

What would it mean to accept Saturn's invitation? To truly do so, we would need not only to fully acknowledge the presence of Saturn's darkness, but also to think about its possibilities. A plea for the Saturnine could address many forms of darkness in our scholarly lives, but here I'd like to consider the anxieties and depressions, both diagnosed and not, that can fall upon us. One contributor writes about the intense isolation and alienation that can accompany emotional distress in our profession:

> The continuing culture of silence is really quite shocking, when you think about it. I felt very ashamed during my graduate school bouts of quite serious depression, and only now do I realize I did not need to be. I was not alone in my experience, but I certainly felt alone — I felt like a freak and a failure. . . . I still feel that I can only really talk about my feelings of insecurity and inadequacy — the well-springs of my depression, when I have it — with my closest friends in the profession, and no one else; everyone expects one to be at the top of your game all the time (or so it feels)
> . . . .

Theseus builds no oratory to Saturn, shows no awareness of the old god's power in his speech about the cosmic *status quo*. In our Thesian moments, we suppress our own freakishness and failure, we ignore or subtly pillory that of others, in order to appear at the top of our game.

What could be a more top-of-the-game enterprise than the *curriculum vitae*? The "course of life" that assembles our thoughts and travels into a coherent story also conveniently omits all hesitations, indecisions, and hardships. There are circumscribed and accepted ways of venting about workload, but if we mention undergoing a period of truly severe distress we risk being "unprofessional."[9] So "unprofessional" are moments of extreme emotional distress that we often take them to be signs that we should leave the field entirely. Several contributors to this essay associate the onset of depression and anxiety with a strong sense of being unfit for our profession:

> My first thought was to drop out. I had never disappointed myself so thoroughly before, and had decided that I was just not cut out for academia.

> I seriously thought of giving up entirely on academia at that point. I entered into a period of depression that has persisted in some small form to the present day, often with periods of greater intensity.

> The Middle Ages were too hard, I wasn't smart enough, I could never do it, I was full of despair, I stopped eating, I lost 20 pounds in two months, I couldn't sleep . . . .

At the mention of exile, sleeplessness, and anxiety, we might initially think of turning away from Saturn's cosmic darkness to claim kinship with the lovesick Palamon and Arcite. When exiled, Arcite, after all, cannot eat or sleep, and grows thin and pale (I.1373–1375, I.1358–1368). As one contributor writes, "The feelings of abandonment, estrangement, and pessimism that run through [the *Knight's Tale*] all resonate with the experience of depression." Our experiences are certainly as

---

[9] Margaret Price makes a similar point about personality traits in the academy: "A certain amount of *acceptable* weirdness (usually called 'quirkiness') does prevail within each discipline or field, of course, but overall, if someone can't hold an engaging conversation over dinner, she is far less likely to succeed as an academic" ("It Shouldn't Be So Hard").

intense and harrowing as those of the characters we discuss dispassionately in class. We lose it entirely:

> I have become insomniac (which doesn't help with the depression) because my brain cannot stop. I cannot stop thinking about the next day's classes, the papers to mark, the students' problems or needs, their mental health or readiness, the administrative things coming up, or family things (I'm the breadwinner for my husband and two children).

> I was to give a talk at a division-sponsored panel at MLA; I had interviews lined up at prestigious schools. And then I found that I couldn't breathe. I started sobbing nonstop. I couldn't sleep, then I couldn't eat, then I couldn't leave my apartment, then I couldn't even stand up.

But while the symptoms may resemble each other, our darknesses are different. A contributor points out a crucial distinction between our experiences and the lovesickness of the knights in the tale:

> Lovesickness has all the right symptoms (lack of ability to eat, sleep, socialize, etc.) but it also has both an identifiable origin and a social/narrative function. Lovesickness stalls Arcite and Palamon for a bit, but it also gives them a path to pursue. I'm not entirely sure I would say the same of depression. I don't know that depression makes "sense" — either logical or perceptual. . . . The condition is stubbornly resistant to narrative closure and even to analysis.

If only we *were* Palamon and Arcite, instead of ourselves. The knights weep heroically; their suffering pushes the narrative forward. If we look for a professional analogy, the knights' early sufferings represent not true Saturnine darkness but rather the socially acceptable and glamorized stereotypes of mental distress associated with the intellectual life: the lonely and isolated scholar, the broody dreamer, the melancholy genius.[10] Adopting one of these theatrical personas is not an acceptance of the Saturnine, just a sneakier path into well-polished Thesianism. The real cold, dark, thinking falls on us like the tower onto the "mynour" tunneling under it; it is more like Arcite's death pangs, not his operatic love-suffering; it has no glamor and it has no apparent use:

> Despair is a smaller emotion: it doesn't burst out and ruin a civilization. It destroys by nibbling, or it falls on you like a weight (a big black dog on your shoulders) and makes you smaller, too: anxiety, literal narrowness, as all your thought and being contracts to consideration of one thing, insomnia as your mind circles and circles, the thinning as your appetite disappears, though you're weighted down by this thing on your shoulders, in your head, in your heart . . . .

> Life with him was a mad dance for which the steps were always changing. So, when I read Chaucer's description of Saturn I am reminded of the chaotic world in which I lived. In the margins of my Riverside edition from graduate school, I have marked this passage with the words "my chaos." I recognized not only the competing impulses and contraries pulling me in two directions, I also recognized the world where what seems to be true turns out to be false.

> The worst part of Depression is the fact that your illness is invisible. Countless times, I have submitted myself to bloodwork and other such medical tests, in the hope that they can find something real to diagnose me with. . . . No, I have Depression . . . that invisible,

---

[10] Individual genius and melancholy started to be strongly associated with each other in the early modern period, according to Panofsky, Klibansky, and Saxl (241–254).

lingering, ultimately untreatable pain that disconnects you from your life and turns you into an observer, albeit one who is still responsible for the subject's behavior and academic progress. Even on my best days, I am standing outside myself, unable to control the hours of unproductive staring at the wall, and in the rare moments when I am allowed to reenter, it becomes painfully clear that I was only allowed back inside because observers cannot produce tears. Once the crying ends, I am banished again, forced to sit still and watch my life go nowhere.

The incomprehensibility and unmanageability of our distress matches the elusiveness and unknowability of Chaucer's Saturn. The old god is difficulty personified, a force that defines itself and isn't created by, or subjected to, human knowledge. The tale's presentation makes this clear. Venus and Mars, the desire and aggression of the tale, are tangible and visible in their oratories, their human-like bodies richly detailed (I.1918–2050).[11] Of Saturn, we see nothing; he is only his own voice, speaking in the darkness.[12] Like the disasters he presides over, Saturn is beyond human comprehension. Saturn embodies the themes that V. A. Kolve identifies in the *Knight's Tale*: "epistemological and teleological darkness" and "human limitation."[13] Saturn's distant path through the cosmos carries in its wake "moore power than woot any man" (I.2455).

Yet it is in Saturn's incomprehensibility that we can see a glimmer of his promise. Ancient and medieval descriptions of Saturn are extremely messy, a flux of different traditions, but one consistent point is that Saturn is depicted as wise as well

---

[11] On Venus and Mars as desire and aggression, see Gaylord, 180.

[12] The tale tells us only that Saturn is "pale" and "colde" (I.2443). On this point, see Leicester's observation that the tale gradually leaves aside personification (316–317).

[13] Kolve, 123, 86.

as harmful.[14] Neoplatonists, in fact, revered Saturn for his power to inspire contemplation.[15] This Saturnine intellect can be seen in Chaucer's tale — a description of Saturn's "olde experience" and "wysdom" precedes his horrible monologue, and the god is paradoxically disastrous and effective. Along with an acceptance of Saturnine darkness, we can explore the potential of Saturnine epistemology.[16] Saturn's challenging and disastrous way of knowing might offer a way of being for a restlessly searching future humanities. Better the contemplative Saturn as a model for scholarship than the commodified Mercury or the power-hungry Jupiter. Medieval tradition associates Mercury with clerkly knowledge, but, as the Wife of Bath points out, such Mercurial clerks can be self-content and prudish (III.697–710). Jupiter, also, is associated with scholars, and the Jupiter-like Theseus propounds a kind of assuring, self-content scholarly theory of a human-directed universe in his well-known speech.[17] We can hold up Saturn as a god of thoughts that aim for a scope beyond the human, that aim for recognition of all forces of the universe, and all the things we feel, without explanation or apology. Saturn as a god of the mystic darkness of contemplation, a patron of critical theory, of relentlessly questioning readings.

We are, after all, people committed to the study of lives, of events, of works of art, of matters of uncertainty, not clerks or

---

[14] Minnis, 140. For Saturn traditions, I rely on Klibansky, Panofsky, and Saxl.

[15] Klibansky, Panofsky, and Saxl, 151–159.

[16] Here I see a possible affinity with Eileen Joy's mention of "sadness and melancholy as forms and signs of deep ecological connections" in her weblog post "Beowulf in the Dark, Medieval Madness, and Blue: Some Items of Possible Interest," In the Middle, July 6, 2011: http://www.inthemedievalmiddle.com/2011/07/beowulf-in-dark-medieval-madness-and.html.

[17] Kolve points out Theseus's link to scholarship (127). Aers notes the inadequacy of Theseus's thinking, pointing out Theseus's lack of philosophical depth and his self-interested use of a simplistically treated "metaphysical language" (195). On the "anthropocentric" nature of the Knight's Tale, see Rudd.

rulers who expect quick results. Aranye Fradenburg elo-
quently advocates careful consideration of medievalists'
emotional investment in our scholarship. She encourages us
to develop "a working awareness of how [our] own to relation
to history could help [us] design important new questions that
could change what counts as knowledge about the Middle
ages or how such knowledge is made."[18] Could we try to see
our most unprofessional and Un-Thesian feelings, our distress
and chaos, as a way in to Chaucer? Not as a glorying in
suffering, but as a recognition of shared fragility? The parade
of disasters in Saturn's speech is, for all its darkness, a spur to
contemplation of connections between the present and the
past. It has some of the most closely grouped oblique
historical references in *The Canterbury Tales*, and can be
taught to students as an aggregate of the disasters that
structure Chaucer's lifetime: the "pestilence" of the Black
Death, the "fallyng of the toures and of the walles" in siege
warfare in the Hundred Years' War, the "cherles rebellyng" of
1381, the "derke tresons" of feuding factions, the "stranglynge
and hangyng by the throte" of Chaucer's one-time associate
Thomas Usk, dangling from the gallows.[19] The point is not
that this passage is merely a coded allegory of historical
events; rather, the lived experience of Chaucer's time distills
itself into the dark poetry of this passage and then
redistributes itself out towards our own time, shaped by our
own understanding of disaster.[20] We know what Saturn does
to us these days. Gillian Rudd observes that Saturn's speech

---

[18] Fradenburg, *Sacrifice Your Love*, 74.

[19] These historical connections are well known, thanks especially to
the comprehensive and well-known historicist Chaucerian scholarship of the late twentieth century, e.g. by Lee Patterson and David
Wallace. Paul Strohm's work, as well as being central to this
enterprise in general, has been crucial for our understanding the
Chaucer-Usk connection; see, for example, Paul Strohm, *Hochon's
Arrow* (Princeton: Princeton University Press, 1992), 145–160.

[20] Butcher and Brown observe that Saturn's speech draws both on
"the general and the particular," and they match Saturn's speech to
various events in Chaucer's time (224–226).

"could almost serve as a description of current ecological warnings," something like the terrible litany mentioned by Timothy Morton: "The sky is falling, the globe is warming, the ozone hole persists; people are dying of radiation poisoning and other toxic agents; species are being wiped out, thousands per year; the coral reefs have nearly all gone."[21] Disaster, in its combination of human and nonhuman elements, of individual subjects and larger networks, is a medium through which communication across time can occur. Of course, we don't want to become humorless mourners, and we don't want to take up the musty posturings of the romanticized scholar. But could there an honest way of noting our special attunement to the unhinging Saturnine chaos of thinking across time? These resonances of Saturn with a distinctively destabilizing kind of knowledge suggest there are intellectual, as well as ethical, reasons for us to be open about the basic realities of our very non-Thesian professional lives.

But the more vague philosophical benefits of Saturnine thinking seem ridiculously abstract right now when we cannot even be open about the everyday darknesses. In the most striking similarity among the testimonials anonymously contributed as material for this essay, the contributors (who did not know each other's identities or consult with each other) identified a pervasive stigmatization of emotional distress in the academy, a stigmatization even of doubt or lack of confidence. Many expressed extreme caution about sharing their experiences of mental distress at all, and most of them observed that the professional academy actively discouraged such discussion. "I feel deeply uncomfortable," one contributor writes, "describing these or any related issues in a professional context. I have felt that discussing mental health. . .would create more problems than it solved." This contributor goes on to say that other students advised that "mentioning the problem would create a stigma I would have

---

[21] Rudd, 64. Timothy Morton, *Ecology Without Nature: Rethinking Environmental Aesthetics* (Cambridge, Mass.: Harvard University Press, 2007), 10.

to grapple with throughout my career." This pattern continues in other contributions. None of us feel comfortable:

> I would not feel at all comfortable talking to colleagues about this . . . .

> I feel very ill at ease discussing mental health issues with anyone who is not in a similar professional position as I am, e.g. graduate student or recent graduate student who has finished. I would not discuss the issue with any full faculty members, especially if they are in any position of influence over me (from my department or in terms of professional networking) . . .

> I have discussed mental health issues with my teachers and mentors, but only when it is relevant to my academic progress, and always with disheartening results.

And why? Because somehow admitting to distress would lessen our reputation:

> [I]n a profession where our judgement is not only always necessary but always being challenged . . . it would be hard to admit to one's flawed vision; one cannot risk being thought untrustworthy, can one?

> I've tried every possible explanation that I can come up with, and yet, I still get the sense that my teachers believe that I am just lazy, or making excuses, or whatnot.

And how ridiculous, given what we study:

> I feel there is an awful lot of unexamined and unrecognized privilege that exists amongst far too many employed academics, whether tenured or on their way to becoming tenured, or even those who

> aren't there yet, but have been continuously employed.
> . . . So many modern medievalists are fond of looking
> at queer theory, monster theory, notions of abjection,
> and so forth from a distanced, ironic, and intellectual
> standpoint, while ignoring the queer, the monster, and
> the abject sitting in the front row taking notes on their
> papers.

As Margaret Price puts it, "It shouldn't be so hard." Price, writing for the web periodical *Inside Higher Ed*, argues that academia retains a (Thesian) view of professionalism narrowly defined as a mastery of congeniality in social situations. Price observes that this focus on professionalism is particularly difficult for academics with diagnosed mental disabilities, but is demoralizing and destructive for everyone in the profession. Price asks us to re-think what we consider professional, to create an academy in which all of us are more open about our distresses, anxieties, and insecurities. We must, Price concludes, "questio[n] the very foundations of academe, our relentless use of social spaces to test scholarly merit, our continued valorization of what Quintilian called 'the good man speaking well.'"[22]

The goal should be a re-evaluation of professionalism, not a disregard for it altogether; certainly our shared enterprise requires dependability, loyalty, generosity, hard work; those who employ us, take our classes, and read our work deserve our full engagement. But if we are to commit ourselves truly to the study of the past, to the study of the humanities, what can we really gain from the Thesian good man speaking well? Is the buttoned-down, impersonal professionalism suited to profit-driven business enterprises a good fit for our wider, stranger enterprise of shared inquiry? Our very strength, our very expertise, comes from darkness, indeterminacy, unmarketably disastrous historical realities, hanging, drowning, plague, ruin. Strange dark Saturnine knowledge, and all the unsightly darkness that goes with it. Let's see with our flawed

---

[22] Price, "It Shouldn't Be So Hard."

vision, be happy with less than enough, and work darkly and beautifully at the bottom of our game.

Because darkness is not always what it seems. For all the darkness in *The Knight's Tale*, when the grove is destroyed for Arcite's funeral it is the *light* that is horrible. When the trees have been cut down, the ground itself, "nat wont to seen the sonne bright," becomes "agast . . . of the light" (I.2931–2932). [23] In another example of dark counter-thinking, movingly discussed by David Aers, Arcite achieves his greatest triumph when, broken in body, dying, beyond all hope of chivalric victory or display, he speaks to Emelye and Palamon and "affirms incarnate human love and friendship even as he fully experiences and acknowledges the miserable precariousness of human life" (I.2743–2797). [24] If our halls and offices, our conferences and classrooms, are not a place for honestly and lovingly being together in all of our own darknesses, then there is no hope left in this world for the unpredictable, transformative, and contemplative gifts of Saturn.

---

[23] Kolve, 131.
[24] Aers, 185.

A Dark Stain and a Non-Encounter

Ruth Evans

I want to write about Alcyone's dream because it's fascinated me for so long, but the pages of my Riverside Chaucer won't stay open at The Book of the Duchess, *so I bend back the spine and put my left palm down firmly on the gutter, but it's as if the book is resisting my desire to read, which annoys me because I'm excited to work out why I find her dream so dark. I know that the trigger will be certain enigmatic words that tease me or some other text that swims into my head as I'm reading. I don't know exactly what that will be, though I remember that the word "derk" is there in the poem somewhere. Now I'm skimming the opening lines, trying to take it in slowly, how the dark dream is introduced, but my eye is racing ahead, anticipating "derk," and although I want this experience to be frictionless, I'm stopping and starting, trying to find a rhythm for my reading, seizing at words and images and dropping them or busily storing them for future recall, and then there it is! Morpheus's cave is "derk as helle-pit." I slow down. Here's the dream. It's as odd as I remember it.*

§ A DARK STAIN

My dark Chaucerian moment is the botched encounter between King Seys and his wife Alcyone in *The Book of the Duchess*, an encounter that takes place in a dream. I think of this moment as a small anamorphic image, whose distorted shape hovers like a dark stain at the edge of the poem. If I shift position, or turn my book at an angle, the stain becomes magically legible.

Hans Holbein the Younger, *The Ambassadors*, 1533 (National Gallery, London)

Hans Holbein's painting *The Ambassadors* is the classic instance of this play with perspectival vision that so entranced European artists in the sixteenth and seventeenth centuries. In the foreground of the portrait floats a strange, elongated image that resolves itself into a perfectly-drawn skull when the viewer stands at a certain angle to the picture. Death looms over the portrait's luminous display of worldly power and possessions. In geometral terms, two incompatible spatial orders — rectilinear and curvilinear — inhabit the flat surface of the painting. I can switch between the two spaces at will, making one image rise up as the other falls away, and vice versa.

But something more than an optical illusion is at stake in the anamorphic game. When the distorted image — the skull — appears whole, the rest of the picture looks fuzzy. The viewer is forced to recognize that the portrait is an illusion: not a world but a set of signifiers. This detaching of the gaze is like the effect of castration. Anamorphosis disturbs my relation to the object, to what is represented, by projecting another reality hidden behind illusionistic space.[1] As Parveen Adams puts it, "A gap opens up between the register of the object and the register of the Real."[2] The Real is ab-sense, the impossibility of sense, but it is also sex, which Lacan designates "lack-of-sex-sense."[3] Sex is senseless, not in the sense that it is meaningless but in the sense that sex is not a relation but the impossibility of a relation. *The Book of the Duchess* ostensibly consoles Chaucer's patron John of Gaunt for the loss of his beloved wife Blanche, whose death was the occasion for the poem. I suggest that Alcyone's dream performs the anamorphic trick of showing another reality behind the space of the poem: the failure of the sexual relationship. (No one said this would be cheerful.)

Lacan's metaphors for perspectival distortion allude precisely to sexual difference. The warped fantasm in Holbein's picture takes "a rising and descending form";[4] the moment when it assumes its rightful dimensions, its

---

[1] Jacques Lacan, *The Ethics of Psychoanalysis: The Seminar of Jacques Lacan, Book VII, 1959-1960*, ed. Jacques-Alain Miller, trans. Dennis Porter (New York: W.W. Norton, 1992), 141; Parveen Adams, *The Emptiness of the Image: Psychoanalysis and Sexual Differences* (London: Routledge, 1996), 112–115, 128. For a study of anamorphosis in premodern literature, see Jen E. Boyle, *Anamorphosis in Early Modern Literature: Mediation and Affect* (Farnham: Ashgate, 2010).

[2] Adams, *Emptiness of the Image*, 128.

[3] Jacques Lacan, "L'Etourdit: A Bilingual Presentation of the First Turn," trans. Cormac Gallagher, *The Letter* 41 (2009): 38 [31–80].

[4] Lacan, *Ethics of Psychoanalysis*, 142.

"developed form," is like "the effect of an erection"; we glimpse, Lacan says, "something symbolic of the function of the lack, of the appearance of the phallic ghost."[5] The phallic metaphors are tiresome because women also have a relation to lack, to castration.[6] But the woman relates to the phallus differently from the man. The man submits to castration, taking as his object of desire *objet a* — not the woman but something in her that is more than is in her — and giving up (Renata Salecl's words) "the hope of finding in his partner his own lack," thus making himself vulnerable to the perception that he is unable to take up his symbolic role: am I a man? can I get it up?[7] The woman, however, struggles with knowing that "she does not possess the object that a man sees in her."[8] This difference, as Salecl argues, relates to the different ways in which the sexual relationship fails for masculine and feminine subjects. Alcyone's dream, I want to argue, concerns not so much her loss of Seys as her tragic experience of the misfiring of the sexual relationship, namely her anxiety about being taken as *objet a*: what does Seys love in me? The register of the Real that Alcyone's dream opens up behind the illusionistic space of the poem invites us to think about disparity in love from the side of the woman. Let us allow this dark stain in the text to assume its proper dimensions.

§ WIFE, CAN'T YOU SEE I'M DROWNING?

Numbed almost to the point of death by a melancholy that has no specified source (love-sickness?) and by lack of sleep, the narrator of *The Book of the Duchess* decides to while away the

---

[5] Jacques Lacan, *The Four Fundamental Concepts of Psycho-Analysis*, ed. Jacques-Alain Miller, trans. Alan Sheridan (London: Penguin, 1977), 86–87.

[6] Adams, *Emptiness of the Image*, 102, 130.

[7] Renata Salecl, "Love Anxieties," in *Reading Seminar XX: Lacan's Major Work on Love, Knowledge, and Feminine Sexuality*, ed. Suzanne Barnard and Bruce Fink (New York: State University of New York Press, 2002), 94 [93–97].

[8] Salecl, "Love Anxieties," 94.

tedium of his *nuit blanche* by reading a book.[9] It works. The narrator is enraptured by Ovid's story of King Ceyx and his wife Alcyone: he finds it "a wonder thing" (61), a source of enchantment, an ironic echo of the decidedly *un*enchanted state in which he began the poem, one of "gret wonder" (1) at still being alive despite his suffering. For Aranye Fradenburg, "sleep, dream, *enchantment*, and memory work all hold out the lure of indifference, of a state in which one will not suffer from one's aliveness."[10] The narrator has shut down his feelings to protect himself from too much reality. Ironically, this reality — that love misses its mark — is exactly what he later tries to get Gaunt's avatar, Man in Black, to *face up to*.

In Chaucer's version of Ovid's tale Seys drowns in a storm at sea, and when he fails to return home, Alcyone is driven crazy . . . by what? By not knowing for certain that he is dead: "'Alas!' quod she, 'that I was wrought! / And wher [whether] my lord, my love, be deed?'" (90–91). Alcyone's animated anxiety is the opposite of the narrator's "astoned" [turned to stone] indifference, his response (presumably) to the pain of unreciprocated love. But it's not that women go mad and men shut down when love goes wrong; rather, each experiences the misfiring of the sexual relation differently.

Alcyone prays to Juno that she may fall asleep and be granted "som certeyn sweven" [an authoritative dream], one that will assure her of the knowledge she craves: "Whether my lord be quyk or ded" (121). Juno grants her prayer, instructing her servant to go to Morpheus, the god of sleep, and to bid him to impersonate Seys: Morpheus must "crepe" [creep, crawl, burrow, enter, steal] (144) into Seys's dead body, and tell "his" wife the truth, straight from the horse's mouth, so to

---

[9] Quotations from *The Book of the Duchess* are from *The Riverside Chaucer*, gen. ed. Larry D. Benson, 3rd edn. (Oxford: Oxford University Press, 1987), cited by line number.

[10] L.O. Aranye Fradenburg, "'My Worldes Blisse': Courtly Interiority in *The Book of the Duchess*," in *Sacrifice Your Love: Psychoanalysis, Historicism, Chaucer* (Minneapolis: University of Minnesota Press, 2002), 91[79–112]; emphasis mine.

speak. Except that the horse is dead. The poem compounds irony on irony: the truth is spoken by an impostor; a lively body is really dead; the god of sleep does not enable Alcyone to go on sleeping but rather wakes her up — and, later, inadvertently kills her. Morpheus here isn't shape-shifting; he is literally crawling inside a dead body. It's a Gothic moment *avant le fait*: Seys's uncanny double is a reanimated corpse that is *creepy*: to be twitching with pain or discomfort, have one's flesh crawl.[11]

I'm marking certain words with a highlighter pen, which slows me down and takes me out of the feeling of being pulled in to the text. Images flash up in my mind's eye: Morpheus creeping into Seys's drowned body, the slack skin draped over him, is a Gustave Doré engraving, morphing into a Vesalius flayed body, lifeless yet prancing. Anamorphosis again! The body as phallus: limp, then swelling up as Morpheus gets inside. It's cruelly ironic: Alcyone hasn't got a husband any more to satisfy her.

Standing by Alcyone's bed in the skin of her dead husband, Morpheus urges her: "Let be your sorwful lyf" (202). But is he asking her to abandon her grief or to put an end to it by killing herself? His words might be comforting — or an incitement to suicide. He then announces: "For certes, swete, I am but ded" (204). Does he mean "I am quite dead," "I am merely dead," or "I am as good as dead"? In Ovid's tale, just as in Guillaume de Machaut's version, Alcyone receives the certain knowledge she craves: "In this way, the beautiful Alcyone clearly saw King Ceyx, and knew without doubt the manner of his passing."[12] But Chaucer's rendering is queasily

---

[11] *Middle English Dictionary*, v. "crepen" (def. 7), http://quod. lib.umich.edu/m/med.

[12] Guillaume de Machaut, *Fountain of Love*, in *Geoffrey Chaucer,*

unresolved. After Morpheus-as-Seys commands Alcyone to bury his body and bids her a loving farewell, Alcyone's reaction is bizarrely confused. Casting her eyes upwards, she sees "noght" (213). Is she still asleep at this point or has she woken up from her sleep? The allusion here might be to the gates of sleep described by Virgil, one of horn, penetrable to vision, and one of ivory, which is opaque. Later medieval dream theorists understand Virgil's interpretation of these two gates as symbolizing two kinds of dream: those that come from outside (that are meaningful) and those that are self-generated and have no meaning.[13] That Alcyone sees "noght" implies that hers is merely an interior dream, signifying nothing. "Allas!" (213) is all Alcyone utters before she faints, and then dies three days later. In Ovid, Juno turns both husband and wife into two halcyon birds whose "love and conjugal vows remain in force."[14] But in Chaucer's account there is no transcendence and no consolation. The 'heterosexual' couple comes to a "dead end."[15]

The narrator's response to this instance of love tragically missing its mark is jarringly insouciant. Earlier, he had displayed a rather showy compassion for Alcyone: "trewely I that made this book / Had swich pitee and swich routhe / To rede hir sorwe, that by my trouthe, / I ferde the worse al the morwe" (96–99). His protestations of sincerity ("trewly"; "by my trouthe"), the repetition of "swich," the emphasis on feelings of "pitee" and "routhe," his empathy for Alcyone in reading about her "sorwe," all constitute a flamboyant, self-fashioning parade of masculine courtly "pitee" for women. But now he is perversely unmoved by her death, claiming that he cannot tell us "what she sayede more in that swow" (215)

Dream Visions and Other Poems: A Norton Critical Edition, ed. Kathryn L. Lynch (New York: W.W. Norton, 2007), 291 [284–299].

[13] Steven F. Kruger, *Dreaming in the Middle Ages* (Cambridge: Cambridge University Press, 1992), 18–19, 21, 75.

[14] Ovid, "The Story of Ceyx and Alcyone," in *Geoffrey Chaucer, Dream Visions and Other Poems*, ed. Lynch, 257 [251–257].

[15] Fradenburg, "'My Worldes Blisse,'" 95.

because it "were to longe for to dwelle" (217). He is impatient
to move on.

Does the narrator's strategic *occupatio* represent a turning
away from the dream's impenetrable kernel — Freud's "navel
of the dream" — or a repeating of it? The narrator returns to
his own situation: had he not read the story, he insists, *he*
would have been "ded, ryght thurgh defaute of slep" (223).
Never mind that both Seys and Alcyone are dead. Their deaths
are lesser events than his own near-death from lack of sleep.
There is a certain aggression in the narrator's jokey dismissal
of Alcyone's plight: why, to stop himself dying from insomnia
he'd be willing to reward Morpheus, or Juno, or anyone —
whatever! — with a luxury bed. The narrative swerve stops us
from inquiring too deeply into the meaning of the dream, but
the tonal shift has the opposite effect: it draws attention to
Alcyone's love-anxiety and to the deaths – and death – of the
loving couple.

§ FATHER, CAN'T YOU SEE I'M BURNING?

I want to put Alcyone's dream in dialogue with another
famous dream of an uncanny reunion following bereavement,
one that concerns not man and wife but a witnessing father
and a sacrificial son: Freud's Dream of the Burning Child.[16]
This juxtaposition looks perverse: although every desire goes
back to a desire of or for the other, the Oedipal motif of
Freud's dream seems remote from the courtly, erotic motifs of
Alcyone's. Yet both dreams speak of an encounter with the
Real — an agonizing intrusion of something "beyond,"
something that marks a limit to knowledge — that makes each
dream the other's double.

In Freud's account, a father has been watching over his
sick child for many days. Once the child has died, the father
lies down to sleep, in view of the body, which is surrounded

---

[16] My terms are from David Lee Miller, *Dreams of the Burning Child:
Sacrificial Sons and the Father's Witness* (Ithaca: Cornell University
Press, 2003).

by candles: "After a few hours' sleep, the father dreams *that the child is standing at his bedside, grasps him by the arm and whispers to him reproachfully, 'Father, can't you see that I am burning?'* He wakes up, notices a bright light coming from the room where the body is lying, hurries over and finds the old attendant fallen asleep, the shroud and an arm of the beloved body burnt by a lighted candle that had fallen across it."[17] For Freud, the dream is a textbook example of wish-fulfillment: it enables the father to prolong his sleep and to see his child alive again.[18]

Yet as Lacan observes, if this dream serves only to satisfy the wish to sleep, then it fulfills a *need*, not a desire.[19] If it fulfilled a need, why would the father awake? What wakes him, in Lacan's words, "is, *in* the dream, another reality," that of the child standing near him, reproaching him for not seeing that he is burning. Isn't this dream, Lacan urges, "an act of homage to the missed reality — the reality that can no longer produce itself except by repeating itself endlessly, in some never attained awakening? . . . the terrible vision of the dead son taking the father by the arm designates a beyond that makes itself heard in the dream. . . . It is only in the dream that this truly unique encounter can occur."[20] The dream speaks of the father's pain at his loss but it also bears witness to a more fundamental loss, one that can never be recovered because it ex-sists outside the phallic order, in "a beyond": the Real. Lacking a signifier, this radical loss makes its searing

---

[17] Sigmund Freud, *The Interpretation of Dreams*, trans. Joyce Crick; Introduction and Notes by Ritchie Robertson (Oxford: Oxford University Press, 1999), 330.

[18] Freud, *Interpretation of Dreams*, 331.

[19] Lacan, *Four Fundamental Concepts*, 57.

[20] Lacan, *Four Fundamental Concepts*, 58. See also Malcolm Bowie, *Lacan* (London: Fontana, 1991), 106: the dream-voice, he says, "is an accident that repeats an accident, an irreducible fragment of the real that speaks of an irrecoverable loss, an encounter that is peremptory and brutal and yet one that can now never, outside dreams, take place."

presence felt in the missed encounter: father and son can never meet again except in a dream.[21]

○

But the words of Seys, the drowned man, aren't like the words of the dead child. They're not urgent or terrible. At times they're comic in their bathos. It's not even his voice. Perhaps that's the point. I'm aware, because it's Morpheus ventriloquizing Seys, that husband and wife are not meeting at all, not even in the dream. The "missed reality" here, the "beyond" that the poem gestures towards in Alcyone's disturbed reaction to the longed-for encounter that misses its mark, is the Real of sexual difference: an irrecoverable loss, lack-of-sex-sense, absex-sense. Is this what Man in Black means when he twice insists to the dumb dreamer "I have lost more than thow wenest" (744, 1138)?

○

Like the child in Freud's dream, Seys bears witness to an unbearable reality: "Ye shul me never on lyve yse' (205) [you will never see me alive] ("Wife, can't you see I'm drowning?"). Yet Alcyone, casting up her eyes, "saw noght" (213). If she sees nothing, the dream comes through the Virgilian gate of ivory and is a mere fantasm, not the truth. But Alcyone also sees nothing because she is not present in the dream. As Lacan says, our position in a dream is "profoundly that of someone who does not see," that is, who is not conscious of herself as

---

[21] As Yün Peng observes, in "A Knock Made for the Eye: Image and Awakening in Deleuze and Freud," in *The Dreams of Interpretation: A Century Down the Royal Road*, eds. Catherine Liu, John Mowitt, Thomas Pepper, and Jakki Spicer (Minneapolis: University of Minnesota Press, 2007), 217 [215–224]: "the dream is not a representation; it is rather a placeholder for something that is not present. This something is the real."

dreaming.[22] The subject slides away. Alcyone is captured by nothing. This is also like the anamorphic effect: the detachment of the gaze annihilates the subject by puncturing the illusion of the world of which the anamorphic stain is a part.

Far from preserving the idea of the loving couple or celebrating the One of erotic fusion, Alcyone's dream speaks of an intolerable anxiety about the sexual relation on the part of the feminine subject. This anxiety has its counterpart (experienced from the side of the man) in the male narrator's "sorwful ymagynacioun" (14), in his anxiety about his insomnia, in his eight-year sickness that can only be cured by one "phisicien" (39) — and it also has its counterpart in Man in Black's anxiety about White's death and his dysfunctional aristocratic identity. Alcyone's dream, in its senselessness, speaks of the impossibility of making sex-sense: masculine and feminine subjects cannot complete each other because they are negated and included in the phallic function in different ways. Alcyone struggles to understand what she represents for Seys, whether she is still the *objet a* around which his fantasies revolve.[23] The narrator, conversely, is "traumatized by not being able to assume his symbolic role"[24] as bearer of the phallus: he is so fearful of disappointing his lady that he has anaesthetized himself: "I have felynge in nothing" (11).

Like Alcyone and like the narrator, Man in Black is in a limbo of living death, a version of Giorgio Agamben's *homo sacer*, the man who can be killed with impunity but not sacrificed. He is "[a]lway deynge and [is] not ded" (588), suspended between death and a terrible aliveness.[25] He is the very image of sorrow: "For y am sorwe, and sorwe ys y" (597). Man in Black moves in a world of mirror-images,

---

[22] Lacan, *Four Fundamental Concepts*, 75.

[23] Salecl, "Love Anxieties," 94–95.

[24] Salecl, "Love Anxieties," 93.

[25] Giorgio Agamben, *Homo Sacer: Sovereign Power and Bare Life*, trans. Daniel Heller-Roazen (Stanford: Stanford University Press, 1998).

identifications and reciprocities: the scene, to borrow Malcolm Bowie's words from another context, "of a desperate delusional attempt to be and remain 'what one is' by gathering to oneself ever more instances of sameness, resemblance and self-replication." But Man in Black enjoys this stasis. He wants to be stuck; he seeks "to remove himself from the flux of becoming."[26] The strange obtuseness of the dreamer in not understanding Man in Black's inexplicable loss powerfully suggests that what is a dream for the narrator becomes as it were Man in Black's dream: that which allows his trauma to emerge repeatedly. In this sense the poem moves from the realm of the imaginary to the realm of the symbolic: rather than dissolving the otherness of Man in Black by becoming his mirror-image, the narrator seeks to engage him as a courtly subject and to move him beyond his stuckness.[27]

Alcyone's dream of a terrifying and deathly non-communication alerts us to a deeper trauma that is at the heart of the poem: that of the Real of sexual difference. In Joan Copjec's words, "To say that the subject is sexed is to say that it is no longer possible to have any knowledge of *him* or *her*. *Sex serves no other function than to limit reason, to remove the subject from the realm of possible experience or pure understanding.* . . . sex, in opposing itself to sense, is also by definition opposed to relation, to communication."[28] Guess why this might not be a good thing for Chaucer to say to the person for whom he wrote this poem, his powerful patron John of Gaunt, Duke of Lancaster, mourning the death of his beloved wife Blanche? It requires, shall we say, a certain tact, a certain delicacy. What is remarkable is that Chaucer rises to the almost impossible task of writing a love letter to a dead woman on Gaunt's behalf while simultaneously acknowledging the impossibility of a sexual relationship through the poem's unfolding of a series of missed encounters: the

---

[26] Bowie, *Lacan*, 92.

[27] Bowie, *Lacan*, 92.

[28] Joan Copjec, "Sex and the Euthanasia of Reason," in *Supposing the Subject*, ed. Joan Copjec (London: Verso, 1994), 21 [16–44].

dreamer's with his "physicien," Alcyone's with Seys, Man in Black's with Blanche. [29] The impossibility of Alcyone constituting Seys's "whole" does not, however, point to the woman's frailty or culpability: rather, lacking a limit, she represents "the failure of the limit, not the cause of the failure."[30]

---

[29] For a psychoanalytic reading of *The Book of the Duchess* that downplays the conventional reading of the poem as "an elegiac love-poem that has found a way to express the lovelorn grief of another" to concentrate on a reading of the dreamer as "the projection of a single, albeit riven, consciousness that is seeking some form of 'other' that will address, perhaps even cure, his own sense of fragmentation and self-alienation," see Peter W. Travis, "White," *Studies in the Age of Chaucer* 22 (2000): 39 [1–66].

[30] Copjec, "Sex and the Euthanasia of Reason," 35.

Chaucerian Afterlives
Reception and Eschatology

Gaelan Gilbert

> To be medieval is to posit a future in the very act of self-recognition,
> to offer a memory or memorial to a future that will be recognized at a
> time and place not yet known.
> ~Andrew Cole and D. Vance Smith, *The Legitimacy of the Middle
> Ages: On the Unwritten History of Theory*

§ PROSPECTUS: BUT DARKLY

The claim of this *essai* is that *Chaucer is eschatological.* I use
this rather specific term first in order to indicate the
apocalyptic aspect of Chaucer's late-medieval theological
context of the four last things (*eschata*) — death, judgment, hell
and heaven — and secondly to illumine a dynamic of textual
dispossession at work in Chaucer's anticipations of reader
response, and of his and his texts' interconnected 'afterlives.'
These dense formulations will require some unpacking, but at
this point it suffices to say that an orientation to the prospect of
future evaluation conditions in advance the "dark" moments
explored below.

Any discussion of eschatology seems for us moderns (even
modern medievalists) to be something of a dark topic, and in
at least two ways. One is the popular darkness associated with
divine judgment, an anxiety nowadays often stripped of any
theological reference whatsoever. Another sense is that
analogous to the Pauline "we see now in a mirror but darkly,"
or *videmus nunc per speculum in enigmate* (1 Cor. 13:12),

simply the fact that we cannot see beyond the mortal bounds of this life, except obscurely in figures. And that kind of obscurity makes the prospect of judgment sometimes hard to bear. The *Cloud*-author alludes to our limits in just these terms:

> For when I sey derknes, I mene a lackyng of knowyng; as alle thing that thou knowest not, or elles that thou hast forgetyn, it is derk to thee, for thou seest it not with thi goostly ighe. And for this skile it is not clepid a cloude of the eire, bot a cloude of unknowyng, that is bitwix thee and thi God.[1]

In a historical eschatology, the dark "cloude of unknowyng" is thus the condition of finitude in temporal existence that qualifies all preparation for either death or the apocalyptic advent of the *eschaton*. In a hermeneutic eschatology pertaining to the afterlife of texts (reception, reader-response and pragmatic rhetorical effect), such "derknes" is inscribed into the event of the text itself as the ambiguous and active medium between other temporalities and agencies. Unlike historical eschatology, in which judgment is deferred until a final singular consummation, there are manifold hermeneutic afterlives, each partially fulfilling the anticipations of an authorial past even while disseminating toward new unforeseen interpretations and exaptations.[2] Thus in my use of "dark," I hope to evoke not only cognitive finitude and anxiety about merit but also the two contexts of future judgment, human and divine, within which agents — authors, characters, readers — confront such "derknes."

In what follows, then, I shall explore in four of Chaucer's

---

[1] *The Cloud of Unknowing,* ed. Patrick J. Gallacher (Kalamazoo: Medieval Institute Publications, 1997), IV.415–419.

[2] For more on exaptations, see Conor Cunningham, *Darwin's Pious Idea* (Grand Rapids: Wm. B. Eerdmans, 2010), 94.

texts enunciations and depictions of Bakhtinian answerability[3] as they emerge by way of embedded readers from the eschatological nexus of the four last things (*eschata*).[4] Again, this concise wording will gain added clarity in light of what follows. It is a matter of becoming sensitized to the dialectic of agency, to the mediation between self and other operative in textuality through temporal distension and distantiation. Chaucer's own sensitivity to the future poses a unique challenge to modernity's "addiction to futurity"[5] in this sense because as Chaucer's readers we ourselves embody the potential futures anticipated by his texts, however unrecognizably, even while we put those texts to present uses. The principal question is: how do contemporary readings coincide or conflict with the forward-directed aspects of texts concerned with their characters', their readers', and their own futures? Beyond any discussion of a determining authorial intention — for it is precisely the absence of such an intention's efficacy that opens the space for hope or anxiety — this analysis will aim to bump around in the dark, stubbing our critical apparatus on the edges of those obscure futures which furnish the imaginative poetic text.

§ ANTICIPATION & ANSWERABILITY IN *RETRACCIOUNS, HOUSE OF FAME, FRIAR'S TALE,* AND *TROILUS AND CRISEYDE*

---

[3] In Bakhtin's words, "Art and life are not one, but they must become united in myself — in the unity of my answerability": Mikhail Bakhtin, *Art and Answerability: Early Philosophical Essays,* eds. Michael Holquist and Vadim Liapunov (Austin: University of Texas Press, 1990), 2.

[4] The phrase 'embedded reader' comes from Elizabeth Allen and concerns characters whose acts of interpretation within a narrative are exemplary for extra-textual readers. See Elizabeth Allen, *False Fables and Exemplary Truth in Later Middle English Literature* (New York: Palgrave MacMillan, 2005).

[5] Nicholas Watson, "The Phantasmal Past: Time, History, and the Recombinative Imagination," *Studies in the Age of Chaucer* 32 (2010): 3 [1-37].

In his *Retracciouns,* a dying Chaucer[6] effectively becomes his own proto-reader, anticipating the evaluation of his texts and appealing for attentive reception.[7] Because texts have their afterlives in readers whom they "sownen into synne" (*CT* X.1086) or, as the Monk has it, "into honestee" (*CT* VII.1967),[8] authorial answerability strives to account for the effects of textual reception and response even while depending upon those effects for future dissemination (or censorship!). What is more, in gauging the potential responses of future readers of his *Retracciouns*, Chaucer recognizes that he is himself a text whom God, as the absolute evaluator, will soon take up and read.[9] In this sense, the Last Judgment constitutes the paradigm of critical assessment and, in a poem like *House of Fame*, provides a speculative backdrop for portraying the arbitrary macrocosm of textual reception that *is* literary history. Both the *Retracciouns* and *House of Fame* portray the composition and dissemination of texts as an especially dangerous form of action, for texts reach far ahead in history to unknown effect. As deeds, the texts produced not only by

---

[6] Melissa Furrow convincingly argues that we should take seriously Gascoigne's fifteenth century reading of the *Retracciouns* as a "deathbed repentance": Melissa Furrow, "The Author and Damnation: Chaucer, Writing, and Penitence," *Modern Language Studies* 23.3 (1997): 252 [245-257].

[7] Furrow is right in her line of reasoning here: "It is not that the fictions are sinful in themselves; it is that they 'sownen into synne,' are conducive to sin; the author cannot trust his readers to use them right. And if the reader does not use them right, the guilt is not just the reader's, but the author's" (250).

[8] All quotations from Chaucer's works are from *The Riverside Chaucer,* gen. ed. Larry D. Benson, 3rd edn. (Oxford: Oxford University Press, 1987); quotations from *Canterbury Tales* (*CT*) cited by fragment and line number, from *Troilus and Criseyde* (*TC*) by book and line number, and *House of Fame* (*HF*) by line number.

[9] Medieval theologians who followed Augustine in *De Civitate Dei* XX-XXII held that the individual judgment of a soul followed immediately after death.

Chaucer but all authors will thus need to be accounted for "at the day of doom" (*CT* X.1092).

Chaucer begins his *Retracciouns* by distributing the agency of both human and divine authorship as contingent upon the response of readers:

> Now I preye to hem alle that herkne this litel tretys or rede, that if ther be any thyng in it that liketh them, that therof they thanken oure Lord Jhesu Crist, of whom procedeth al wit and al goodnesse. / And if ther be any thyng that displease hem, I preye hem also that they arrette it to the defaute of myn unkonnynge and nat to my wyl, that wolde ful fayn have seyd bettre if I hadde had konnynge. (*CT* X.1080–1081)

The careful distinction made between "wyl" and "konnynge" suggests a sophisticated awareness of the psychological faculties involved in questions of merit and salvation. [10] Chaucer accordingly aligns his "entente" (*CT* X.1083) with the Pauline dictum — "'Al that is writen is writen for doctrine'" (*CT* X.1083; Romans 15:4) — commonly invoked by medieval writers to justify the pedagogical worth of narrative fictions (*e.g.* the Nun's Priest's envoy, *CT* VII.3438–3446). [11] By

---

[10] According to late-medieval voluntarism, volition trumped intellect with respect to meriting grace. See Gordon Leff, *Heresy in the Later Middle Ages: The Relation of Heterodoxy to Dissent* (Manchester: Manchester University Press, 1967).

[11] It is worth adding nuance to the notion of "intention" at this point. "Entent" is an Englishing of the Latin rhetorical *intentio,* which describes a work's meaning and structure; "[r]ather than be concerned with an author's individual aims, *intentio,* a prescriptive category, indicates the abstract truth behind a text; in a sense, it thus most closely corresponds not to an inherent property of a work but to a reading practice": Jocelyn Wogan-Browne, Nicholas Watson, Andrew Taylor, and Ruth Evans, "The Notion of Vernacular Theory," in *The Idea of the Vernacular: An Anthology of Middle English Literary Theory, 1280-1520* (University Park: Pennsylvania State University Press, 1999), 328.

locating Paul's flexible hermeneutic principle just prior to his request for prayers, Chaucer situates his entire poetic *oeuvre* within an eschatological milieu, expressing mutual concern over both the merit of his texts for future readers and of himself for God. This is articulated directly at the end, "so that I may been oon of hem at the day of doom that shulle be saved" (*CT* X.1091).

Regarding literary status, of course, Chaucer has long attained beatitude. Yet the very instability of poetic fame forces a deeper question: how are readers of Chaucer's texts responsible for Chaucer as an eschatologically answerable agent? In other words, if reception partially determines the import of texts as deeds, and such deeds — for Chaucer at least — have everlasting repercussions, are critical interpretations of Chaucer's texts somehow reductive in their neglect of this soteriological dimension? Given the postmodern death of the author, of what importance for critical scholarship is the appeal of a dying author?

The fact that eschatological reference is a medieval convention only calls for a *more* serious consideration of similar topoi in medieval literary texts.[12] Yet a Barthesian theoretical persuasion, in failing to consider the pragmatic dynamic of Bakhtinian answerability, seems to permit sustained inattention to such conventional anticipations of death and afterlife like Chaucer's, to the extent that modern readings of the *Retracciouns* typically culminate with a retreat into critical neutrality,[13] or a bland celebration of its internal

---

[12] The suggestion that Chaucer is merely capitalizing on an opportunity to reiterate his *oeuvre* (as he had done in the *Man of Law's Tale* and the prologue to *Legend of Good Women*) seems too crassly to impute ulterior motives to what is, after all, a textual repertoire, but one given with a very specific and sober purpose, if we accept Gascoigne's account. For a suggestion to the contrary, see John M. Bowers, *Chaucer and Langland: The Antagonistic Tradition* (Notre Dame: University of Notre Dame Press, 2007), 161–162.

[13] For an overview of the critical reception of the *Retracciouns,* see J.D. Gordon, "Chaucer's Retraction: A Review of Opinion," *Studies in Medieval Literature in Honor of Albert Croll Baugh,* ed.

contra-dictions.[14] As a result, the linguistic reciprocation that Chaucer assigns — prayer for his soul — grates uneasily with the text's function as an object of critical analysis. Its exposure of Chaucer's potentially genuine post-mortem concerns has for the most part seemed to encourage its qualification as more unfashionably medieval than can be comfortably engaged within the parameters of a modern "collective cultural imaginary."[15] Despite Melissa Furrow's excellent analysis, the *Retracciouns* remain a dark site of ambivalence for Chaucer criticism.

Like us, however, Chaucer was also disenchanted with certain versions of the *eschaton*. Take, for instance, the *House of Fame*. Written about two decades before the *Retracciouns, House of Fame* is Chaucer at his most experimental and audacious. Helen Cooper sees it as the beating heart of Chaucer's anti-Danteism, a chaotic and overdetermined satire of the *Commedia*.[16] Dante's presumption in damning his political enemies is parodied by Fame's mock Last Judgment in Book III, an eschatology as discordant with the biblical "Apocalips" (*HF* 1385) as it is with Dante's exposé of the afterlife. And yet a coincidence of hermeneutic and religious afterlives becomes uniquely visible in this part of *House of Fame*. After Book II ends with a spectacular figuration of a general resurrection, nine categorical groups of utterances are judged of their merit for good fame, the latter functioning

---

MacEdward Leach (Philadelphia: University of Pennsylvania Press, 1961), 81–97.

[14] George Kane speaks of the *Retracciouns* as an "expression of religious submission [that] has embarrassed some critics to the extent of making them want to deny its authenticity or else its sincerity": George Kane, "Langland and Chaucer: An Obligatory Conjunction," *Chaucer and Langland: Historical and Textual Approaches* (London: The Athlone Press, 1989), 33.

[15] Watson, "The Phantasmal Past," 36.

[16] See Helen Cooper, "The Four Last Things in Chaucer and Dante: Ugolino in the House of Rumour," *New Medieval Literatures* 3 (1999): 39–66.

diegetically as a rival version of beatitude. Framed with biblical allusions, Fame exercises her absolute power (*potentia absoluta*) and scandalizes justice by treating like cases differently:

> And somme of hem she graunted sone,
> And some she werned wel and faire,
> And somme she graunted the contraire
> Of her axyng outterly.
> But thus I seye yow, trewely,
> What her cause was, y niste.
> For of this folk ful wel y wiste,
> They hadde good fame ech deserved,
> Although they were dyversely served. (*HF* 1538–1546)

Hermeneutically, Book III depicts an absolute yet radically inconsistent reader, a monstrous bundle of impulsive misreadings (*HF* 2110-17), an author's worst nightmare. But Fame's arbitrariness and caprice as a divine judge inaugurates a bad eschatology without room for post-textual prayers or interpretive mercy, offering an instructive contrast to and even justification for Chaucer's more serious post-mortem concerns in the *Retracciouns*. In Kerby-Fulton's words, "it is as if Chaucer is reenacting in a pagan setting an Ockhamesque nightmare of the Last Judgment gone mad — a Last Judgment, that is, in which *everything* is decided by divine *potentia absoluta* and nothing by *potentia ordinata*."[17] I would even go so far as to argue that *House of Fame* constitutes a sort of Chaucerian-Menippean satire, with its experimental deployment of personification allegory, its affirmation of logical contradiction (*HF* 1025–30, 2088–91), and its speculative, open-ended parody of the frightening extremes of

---

[17] See Kathryn Kerby-Fulton, *Books Under Suspicion: Censorship and Tolerance of Revelatory Writing in Late-Medieval England* (Notre Dame, MI: University of Notre Press, 2006), 346.

voluntarist soteriology, one of the hottest philosophical topics of the fourteenth century.[18]

The response of the narrative persona and embedded reader "Geffrey" (*HF* 729) is one of sympathy with the unjustly condemned, evoking academic terminology with "gilteles" and aligning Fame's arbitrariness with the radical contingency personified by her allegorical sibling Fortune (*HF* 1547):

> "Allas," thoughte I, "what aventures
> Han these sory creatures!
> For they, amonges al the pres,
> Shul thus be shamed gilteles." (*HF* 1631–1634).

Later, not admitting to want fame (a coy authorial move on Chaucer's part), Geoffrey rejects Fame's equivocity, opting to judge — and be answerable only to — himself:

> "Sufficeth me, as I were ded,
> That no wight have my name in honde.
> I wot myself best how y stonde;
> For what I drye, or what I thynke,
> I wil myselven al hyt drynke,
> Certeyn, for the more part,
> As fer forth as I kan myn art." (*HF* 1876–1882).

Like Chaucer in the *Retracciouns*, Geffrey here strives to assume responsibility for his "art" (*HF* 1882) in the face of divine judgment, and we rightly laud his refusal of Fame's decrees as a vernacular *facere quod in se est*. Yet the force of his proto-modern assertion over and against the contradictions of hermeneutic contingency, even if (or

---

[18] See Kathryn Lynch, "The *Parliament of Fowls* and Late-Medieval Voluntarism (Part I)," *Chaucer Review* 25.1 (1990): 1–16, and David Aers, *Salvation and Sin: Augustine, Langland, and Fourteenth-Century Theology* (Notre Dame: University of Notre Dame Press, 2009).

especially when) divine, remains in question. He never wakes up, after all! And while this seems not to bode well for Chaucer's own deathbed anxieties, it is precisely the false immortality stemming from the literary fame of his more bawdy works that Chaucer is rejecting in the *Retracciouns*, hoping for the evaluation of a more consistently compassionate divine judge.

The demonic fiend in the *Friar's Tale* likewise exposes the frightening consequences of interpretive contingency, but to even darker ends. In the tale, a disguised fiend instructs a corrupt summoner in the nuances of speech genres, secretly aiming to secure the summoner's damnation. To carry out his plan, the fiend teaches a voluntarist hermeneutic that his own fluid onto-morphology — "in divers art and in diverse figures" (*CT* III.1486) — can later misappropriate. At the tale's climax, an irate widow who is ignorant of the yeoman's demonic identity invokes the "devel blak and rough of hewe" (*CT* III.1622) in cursing the summoner, whose own willfully unrepentant response enables the fiend (according to his own schematic) to demand from the summoner the literal fulfillment of her figurative condemnation: "And with that word this foule feend him hente; / Body and soule he with the devel wente" (*CT* III.1637–1638). The fiend hopes for the same dark consequences of misreading that Chaucer fears in his *Retracciouns*, ironizing in the summoner the fact that discursive "mysdedes" (*CT* III.1664) *do* determine post-mortem destiny. The tale's conclusion hinges upon not an absolute reader (like Fame) but a metamorphosing one who capitalizes upon linguistic dispossession in order to gain possession of the summoner in the "hous of helle" (*CT* III.1652), described as an infernal academy where hermeneutic "sentence" is read (*CT* III.1515–1520).

In light of the fiend's overdetermination of intentional utterance, the Friar cautions the exercise of readerly agency, inviting a common response derived from the rhetorical efficacy of his exemplary fiction:

"But for to kepe us fro that cursed place,
Waketh and preyeth Jhesu for his grace
So kepe us fro the temptour Sathanas.
Herketh this word! Beth war, as in this cas."
(*CT* III.1653–1656)

In the so-called epilogue of *Troilus and Criseyde* (V.1765–1870), the narrator similarly recognizes the agency of the reader, pleading with his personified text that "non myswrite the" (*TC* V.1795) as he issues it forth into the future: "Go, litel bok, go, litel myn tragedye" (*TC* V.1786). Several lines later, Troilus's soul also issues out of his body, though toward a synoptic celestial position (*TC* V.1807–1810) from which he chortles at living mortals below.

Troilus's laughter continues to be a source of contention for Chaucer criticism, with some scholars arguing for the passage's irony, some for its coherent seriousness. Most helpful for our purposes is a reading of the epilogue as a narration of Troilus's very own retraction. Just as Chaucer's *Retracciouns* formally dispossess a textual *corpus* of those works which may promote "worldly vanitees" (*CT* X.1085), so Troilus, after his soul is dispossessed of its textually constituted body, revokes with disdain the "worldly vanyte" (*TC* V.1837) of his former "blynde lust" (*TC* V.1824). And yet he betrays no evidence of being repentant or of assuming responsibility. Speech acts evidently bear less ethical weight for Troilus, whose rhetorical coercion of Criseyde (via Pandarus) — a serious linguistic "mysdede" — has no clear eschatological repercussions. Quite the opposite, in fact: Troilus is taken up into celestial immortality, the only character among those we have examined who *may* attain a good afterlife, depending on the pagan gods' (arbitrary?) decision. Chaucer's anticipation of future readers, on the other hand, articulates a more nuanced and risky understanding of answerability than Troilus' scorn of "al oure werk" (*CT* V.1823). Chaucer seems to have internalized the answerability that is bound up with any exercise of linguistic agency. Far from assuming Troilus' proud stance, in the

Retracciouns he accepts blame and shuns praise, acknowledging (at least rhetorically) the co-implication of his own and his readers' futures.

With reflexive texts like the *Retracciouns* or the *Troilus* epilogue, authorial answerability seems to operate like an ideal target which multiple and sometimes conflicting vectors aim to hit: who *is* answerable, and to what degree, in any given speech act or text-event? The response is necessarily contingent on the circumstantial details born out in the figurative complexity and moral ambiguity of linguistic communication. Chaucer's yielding of *Troilus* to the scrutiny of "moral Gower" and "philosophical Strode" (*TC* V.1856, 1857) "to correcte / of youre benignites and zeles goode" (*TC* V.1858–1859), for instance, can be read as hoping for the possibility of good constructive reception even while privileging certain readers over others. Chaucer thereby expands the scope of his potential audience — whose response determines the quality of his own textual agency — by intertwining historical and hermeneutic afterlives; after earlier begging of his text "that thow be understonde, God I biseche!" (*TC* V.1798), he prays for universal divine reception: "So make us, Jesus, for thi mercy, digne" (*TC* V.1868). However conventional, such universal(ist) appeals traverse historical distance to include *all* possible readers, presupposing a robust notion of answerability hinged on the future divine judgment as itself a reading of infinite scope, made from an absolutely intimate vantage.

§ EPILOGUE: OR EPITAPH

Although the Monk prefaces his *de casibus* tragedies by anticipating their readerly afterlife of inciting "honestee" (*CT* VII.1967), he never finishes telling them. The Knight, otherwise a paragon of bravery, quails before the darkened countenance of Fortune (Fame's sister, remember) and interrupts: "I seye for me, it is a greet disese / Wheras men han been in greet welthe and ese, / To heeren of hir sodein fal, allas!" (*CT* VII.2771–2773). This finicky yet forced foreclosure provides yet another example of embedded misreading alongside caprice (Fame), autonomy (Geffrey), malice (the fiend), and scorn (Troilus).

The *Retracciouns* seem to trouble all of these dark receptions — retrospectively qualifying an entire literary *oeuvre* in the process — by exposing Chaucer's (un)dying hope in the possibility of good readings and good readers. If Gascoigne's account of the occasion of their composition is accurate, Chaucer's *Retracciouns* reveal an author suspended between multiple contingent finite judgments within history and a final, eschatological evaluation beyond all misappropriation (but not figuration). Yet as with textual interpretation, so the results of the final divine critique can themselves be partially determined by the "multiplicacioun" (*HF* 784) by others of a certain mode of response that acknowledges, beyond all failure of nerve, the shared vulnerability of finitude. And it is just such a "wounded"[19] mode of response, namely prayer, that Chaucer begs from us: "Wherfore I biseke yow mekely, for the mercy of God, that ye preye for me that Crist have mercy on me and foryeve my giltes; / and namely of my translacions and enditynges of worldly vanitees, the whiche I revoke in my retracciouns" (*CT* X.1083–1084).[20]

While this articulation places a burden of action upon us, such requests can be ignored or denied. We are inclined to pass off the distantiated appeal as vacuously conventional, laden with ironic ulterior motivation, or as an impersonal semiotic patterning available to us only after the death of the author (both metaphorical and literal), and therefore of no real consequence for the entity that was once the efficient cause of the *Canterbury Tales*, a composite of body and soul,

---

[19] Jean-Louis Chretien, "The Wounded Word: Phenomenology of Prayer," *Phenomenology and the Theological Turn: The French Debate,* ed. Dominique Janicaud, trans. Bernard G. Prusak (New York: Fordham University Press, 2000), 176–216.

[20] Among the revoked texts, significantly, are our three texts of interest: "the book of Troilus; the book also of Fame . . . the tales of Canterbury, thilke that sownen into synne" (*CT* X.1085).

with children and even a proper name: Geoffrey Chaucer. Given all sorts of larger contextual differences, moreover, like our inhabiting a post-Christian cultural (or at least academic) milieu, perhaps we are not able to do otherwise, thus precluding certain types of reader response *tout court.*

If this is the case, then we rather awkwardly find ourselves as addressees of a most urgent plea at an intersection of historical and hermeneutic vectors: one, an imperative from the medieval past attempting to anticipate its own afterlives; the other, an interpretive response in the present facilitated through informed, disinterested retrospection. Of course, unlike that of the enthroned judge of the Johannine Apocalypse, both perspectives are limited, and yet there is a sense that we embrace the "derknes" of history with more ease because of an assurance of our status as the unimaginable future of any past perspective that we may select as an object of scholarly interest. In thus neglecting the full weight of Heidegger's sense of *inter-est*, do we not sometimes derive strange solace in seeing the expectant medieval gaze fall short?

I aim here to tease out a certain dark ethos tempting for those — like myself — who presume to wield the critical gaze, and to wonder: can dead authors be candidates for the ethical Other? If, as Bakhtin stresses, every act "is truly real . . . only *in its entirety*"[21] (and texts are never-finished acts, always open to new receptions and readings) then must our answerability as writers really only be to posterity and not to the past, not also to those who are — and felt themselves to be — answerable *to* us, as forebears? And yet beyond the apparatus of tradition, how to bear the weight of what has already been said? This is the other side of Nicholas Watson's point about modernity's collective amnesia and self-definition over and against an archaic, inconsequential, and perhaps necessarily misrepresented past (the *Dark* Ages). Despite or even because of these modern tendencies, it seems timely to venture that we can only become truly answerable in entertaining the possibility of being darkly prefigured by, and thus in some measure

---

[21] See Bakhtin, *Toward a Philosophy of the Act*, 2.

the unwitting fulfillments of, the futures that the past anticipates in us.

Black Gold
The Former (and Future) Age

Leigh Harrison

Despite their pretense of explaining beginnings, creation myths often if not always have ends in mind — a fact that certainly holds true for Chaucer's "Former Age." On the face of it, the poem is *only* a creation myth: its verse tells the story of human community at its origins, of a freer life (with only "good feith the empeirice" [55])[1] before complex estate hierarchies and the State. Its few stanzas have all the look and feel of a sad song whose melody the centuries have worn away, with all the misty revelation of prehistoric "folk" impulse that the "ballad" label still inevitably implies. This obscurity of age in turn lends the poem its own rusty darkness, over and above the darkness of loss that its narrative claims (however dimly) to recover and bring to light. Most readers, including me, encounter "The Former Age" mainly as a poem cataloging and expressing — simply about — great loss.

Yet contrary to first impressions and the precedents of literary history, I suspect, "loss" is not really the poem's main concern (or at least not in the way it would first appear). As its narrative shifts from the pre-history to the "present" day, so does the sense of the knowledge that it offers: "The Former Age" might lament a vanished past on the surface, but in fact (like any creation myth) it does so only to account for

---

[1] All references to Chaucer's poetry are to *The Riverside Chaucer*, gen. ed. Larry D. Benson, 3rd edn. (Oxford: Oxford University Press, 1987), by line number.

contemporary circumstances. As such, even though the poem's simple and haunting form promises to reveal a radiant ancestral *Volksgeist*, its narrative actually retreats from the revelation of history (and even the declaiming narratorial subject, "Chaucer") that we expect. In fact, operating by means of the very techniques that it claims to deplore, it masks values and priorities in which it has cause (through its very existence) to rejoice.

This is no accident. To be effective, "The Former Age" depends on its not being the type of poem — fragmentary, a solitary ancient voice recorded unawares — that it might claim to be. It draws not so much on ancestral, oral memory, as on a richly textual — even classical — memory store to make its claims, which all but explicitly present a return to the *Etas Prima* as impossible and not even particularly desirable. In that case it can even, perversely, be read as an *apologia* (not an apology) for an enthralled, feverish yearning for production it ascribes to Chaucer's time, though the same yearning is not unrecognizable today. Production is not the first term that comes to mind when describing "The Former Age," true, and the defense of production here is not without its tension: the "former" people who are the poem's ostensible heroes neither spin nor toil. In fact a certain horror inheres in the shadowy, laborious descent for metal that catalyzes the change from one age to another. But more than anything else, an inexhaustible potential characterizes the early humans' common life. The urge to build, to create, and to deplete that characterizes even the present day can't be far behind.

Not so much glittering but seeping into view, like oil, the allure of complex estates and competitions helps account for the profound blackness in this apparently simple poem. Commentators have noted that the narrator in "The Former Age" does not praise these first ancestors for their lack of comforts — though why should he, given that they have never given anything up? His assessment seems to waver between disgust and pity for them, instead, as when he describes their sleeping arrangements:

> Yit was no paleis-chaumbres, ne non halles;
> In caves and wodes softe and swete
> Slepten this blissed folk withoute walles,
> On gras or leves in parfit quiete. (41–44)

By the standards of a later era, these are hardly beds at all; but even so (if with a hint of surprise), the narrator describes the early peoples' sleep as profoundly deep and secure:

> Ne doun of fetheres, ne no bleched shete
> Was kid to hem, but in seurtee they slepte.
> Hir hertes were al oon withoute galles;
> Everich of hem his feith to other kepte. (45–48)

What the poem (like its precursors) describes, then, is a past of impossible estrangement from the driven character of the present, not only in its (negative) privation of goods but also its (positive) freedom from anxieties — chief among them that restlessness to fulfill some livelihood perfectly. The lines imply that the earliest people, lacking social anxiety through their inchoate lack of "estates," were on balance far more blessed than ages yet to come.

Just how unavoidably different this first status quo seems for the Chaucer of "The Former Age" — how much not to be looked back to, even as an ideal — appears with special vibrancy when the poem turns toward the subject of the first-peoples' nourishment. For just as there are no hierarchies to distress man, there is likewise no variation or progress between people. The similes immediately turn bestial to describe their utter congruity, so alien to the medieval (and contemporary) social system: they are "lambish people, voyd of ale debat" — and as for the utter blandness of their swinish food,

> Yit nas the ground nat wounded with the plough,
> But corn up-sprong, unsowe of mannes hond,
> The which they gnodded, and eete nat half ynough.

This pigs' food makes a comment on the first humans' standard of productivity — which is none. They "heeld them payed of the food that the ete": but this is no real pay (and there has been no work).

◉

The lack of production at the beginning, however, is not because of a lack of materials to work from. The first peoples' world is literally full of gold, Chaucer tells us, in a trope common to other medieval works (like this twelfth-century poem by the monk Bernard of Cluny):

> Aurea tempora primaque robora praeterierunt
> Aurea gens fuit et simul haec ruit, illa ruerunt.
> Flebilis incipit aurea suscipit aurea metas;
> Transiit ocius et studium prius, et prior aetas.
> Gens erat aurea, cui furor alea, cui scelus aurum,
> Cui pudor emptio, cui necque mentio divitiarum.
> Non erat abdere fas neque tollere lucra crumenis.
> Plenus opum Tagus aurifluus, vagus ibit arenis.
> Moribus aemula lucra pericula quam preciosa,
> Non homo foderat aut fore noverat invidiosa.
> Sumpsit ut aurea ponderra ferrea spicula quisque—
> Mox tumor iraque sustulit utraque pugnat utrisque.

[The Golden Age and primal strengths have perished. The race of gold existed, and once this fell, those too collapsed. The former zeal has swiftly passed away along with the former age. Golden was the race for whom gambling was madness, gold was a vice, buying was shameful, wealth was not even mentioned. To conceal riches, to carry riches in purses was unlawful. The wandering Tagus, full of treasures, flowed with golden sands. Man did not dig for riches, the enemy of mortals, as dangerous as they are precious — nor did he know that they would stir envy. Each man took up weights of iron just as weights of gold; but soon Pride and Wrath raised their spears, and each fights the other.][2]

The connection here of various latencies — sexuality, metal, work itself — is very clear from this analogue; the situations that Bernard and Chaucer both depict, with their opposition between latency and entelechy, are the same.

Chaucer mirrors the *Consolation of Philosophy* with his focus on things "no man" had done yet that mark his entry into full civilization: in contrast to the more upbeat account of things man did for the first time in Virgil's *Georgics*, the phrasing implies risky aberration and a sense of prior emptiness ("no man") in the world. The connotations are probably warranted, however, as nothing the first people of the poem do resembles activities socially organized in terms of profession or the estates so central to the medieval social imaginary. The fact that this state changes — and moreover where it changes in "The Former Age" — is doubly important as a result:

What sholde it han avayled to werreye?
Ther lay no profit, ther was no richesse,
But cursed was the tyme, I dare wel seye,
That men first dide hir swety bysinesse
To grobbe up metal, lurkinge in derknesse,
And in the riveres first gemmes soghte.
Allas, than sprong up al the cursednesse
Of coveytyse, that first our sorwe broghte. (25–32)

---

[2] Ronald Pepin, "Scorn for the World: Bernard of Cluny's *De contemptu mundi*," *Medieval Texts and Studies* 8 (East Lansing: Colleagues Press, 1991), 76–77.

The passage describes here how "man" enters the scene to shift mere "people" into the work of civilization, or at least the path to it, through a type of mining that Chaucer overlays with sexuality: it is "swety bysinesse" that moreover leads to a kind of fertility and fecundity as the "cursednesse of covetyse" "sprong up."

Chaucer heightens the sexuality inherent in the passage with the last line of the stanza, "that first our sorwe broghte" — echoing as it does the medieval Christian sentiment that the sin of Adam and Eve first brought sorrow into the world. In Genesis 3:16, where the word first appears, God tells Eve that "multiplicabo aerumnas tuas et conceptus tuos in dolore paries filios" [3] ["I will multiply thy sorrows, and thy conceptions: in sorrow shalt thou bring forth children"].[4] Chaucer's choice of the adverb "swety" might also be significant: in Genesis, sweat and labor is the price Adam pays for his sin (see Genesis 3:19) — the difference here being that Adam's sin set humans on a path to very poor nourishment won with labor from rocks and thistles, while the labor of men in Chaucer's poem leads to the invention of a series of delicacies that ends the poem.

The Boethian version avoids these scriptural references, by contrast, choosing to note only how the gems that would cause so much trouble "wished" to remain hidden:

> Heu primus quis fuit ille,
> Auri qui pondera tecti
> Gemmasque latere volentes
> Pretiosa pericula fodit? (II.m.5.27–30)

---

[3] *Biblia Sacra: iuxta Vulgatam versionem*, eds. Robert Weber and Roger Grayson (Stuttgart: Deutsche Bibelgesellschaft, 1994).

[4] *The Holy Bible*, translated from the Latin Vulgate and diligently compared with the Hebrew, Greek, and other editions in diverse languages, pref. William H. McClellan, S.J. (New York: Douay Bible House, 1941).

[Alas, who was he who first dug out the weight of covered gold and gems that wished to remain hidden, precious perils?][5]

Despite these oblique references to the Genesis story, however, Chaucer's "Former Age" on the whole joins Boethius' account in not referring to the Bible — even actively, with purpose. Doing so was certainly not difficult: non-Biblical origin narratives circulated even among Christian audiences well into the Middle Ages. In most of these, as in the classics, writers seem to have been concerned to produce an authoritative "historical" account of beginnings — the texts' stated aim — as a complaint against modern vices weighted down with exemplary force. Yet by not allowing the existence in the former age even of classical gods, either, Chaucer's poem seems systematically to deny the "lambish people" any part in a larger a cosmic hierarchy — let alone entry into the larger stream of Biblical salvation narrative:

Yit was not Jupiter the likerous,
That first was fader of delicacye,
Come in this world; ne Nembrot, desirous
To regne, had nat maad his toures hye. (56–59)

With the removal of all divinity from the earlier time he describes, Chaucer further removes his poem's "lambish" protagonists from an important human sphere. They have neither society nor, it seems now, souls; frozen in a present that will tragically lead to *us*, they can neither collaborate nor seem able to aspire.

With their fall, the precipitating discovery of "precious perils" lying within the earth, these not-quite-three-

---

[5] Boethius, *The Consolation of Philosophy*, trans. S. J. Tester, in *Theological Tractates and The Consolation of Philosophy*, eds. and trans. H. F. Stewart, E. K. Rand, and S. J. Tester, Loeb Classical Library (Cambridge: Harvard University Press, 1973); translation mine.

dimensional forbears plunge headlong into the pursuit of endless productivity — an always actualizing, full-throttle economy that "otherworldly" religion would claim to abhor, were it only to exist — and exist it does, as the newer dispensation begins. A lust to make and achieve comes to comprise the center of humanity's suddenly fervid activity; it takes only the small step to inventing gods to temper that will to produce and lend it dignity with the name of a soul.

While the removal of a divine realm from the purview of "The Former Age" isn't necessarily good or bad by itself, then, its anthropological outlook is dark. The disappearance (or non-appearance) of divinity removes from the poem a positive ideal that produces meaning, leaving a vacuum that significance must rush to fill. The stanza's reference to Jupiter and Nimrod, hinting at the classical pantheon and the single Biblical deity, prove symptomatic of the overabundance of a creatively overheated latter age. The poem's easy familiarity with both mythologies evokes and indicts the capacious, eclectic authorial figure we can recognize behind Chaucer's other works.

Not that the figure of the poet — here at least — gives synthesizing order to this very medieval chaos of abundance. No figure or voice seems to take up the ethically orienting role, even though both medieval literature and its theorists understood poets to take part in a sort of prophetic responsibility. Chaucer hardly appears at all, in fact, lurking like dark matter or transparent as a ghost. In his place we have only the ballad's empty lyrics, a small black box resampling earlier text: a voice like mourning in autotune, not quite as recognizably authentic as its subject matter would demand, no doubt because it can only exist due to the tragic circumstances it relates. We might even call the poet here non-human, offering as he does a vision of humanistic discourse diffused only for the sake of societal self-evaluation: a wish for lambs to be men, or robots to pass a Turing test. Such anachronistic similes are appropriate because, in the last analysis, this poem about an irredeemable past is really about the future: a burnished mirror of older tropes reflecting the fragmented society and the even more profoundly competitive, productive, "self-fashioning" age to come.

◉

Perhaps it's best to read all the untapped potential suggested earlier in "The Former Age," then, as part of the same darkness with which the poem ends. The anaphora of deprivation with which this ballad concludes gives way to a surplus — of money, clothing, and food, all markers of the new estates — yet this in turn collapses into another type of negativity: "nis but"

> . . . covetyse
> Doublenesse, and tresoun, and envye,
> Poyson, manslawtre, and mordre in sondry wyse.
> (61–63)

In this ultimate darkness, the poem unveils the effects of all the production it slights the first people for avoiding, showing that the endless creation of new realities from so much past potential effects growth as relentless and deadly as a cancer: the series of foods (beginning with scarcely human "pounage" and ascending to "clarre or sauce of eglantine") concludes, all-too-significantly, with "poyson." The very guarantees and engines of good life conspire to take it away, with those sauces and stocks turning the very mouths that ingest them into dust. After their first transition from vegetables to meat, a shift impossible without increased social stratification, humans even begin to consume each other.

It seems even more sinister, then, that Chaucer should so entirely abandon the reader to the facts of the poem. The impersonal common narrator offers no advice; charming Chaucer "himself" is simply nowhere to be found. Yet though Chaucer seems to hide from these issues in "The Former Age," in another way they seem to have exerted enormous influence on his overall poetic career. *The Book of the Duchess*, for instance, uses as its starting point the same insomnia that bedding, in this poem, was invented to prevent. "The Former Age" arguably exists to draw attention to this symptom — but not, like other nonbiblical creation myths, to label it an avoidable vice. The contour of the poem suggests an irreversible and unavailable transition from the prehistoric golden age to "oure dayes." The impotence of classical poets to suggest a way out — they, also, have come too late — shows off the ravenous, self-defeating impulses of "korving" and "grobbing" that mark the entire poem. If "hevene hath propretee of sikernesse," as another short poem of Chaucer's opines ("Fortune," l. 69), nothing in this poem seems *siker* except the poem itself.

It may be best to read the fact of this poem as a sort of puzzle, one that puzzles mainly because we call it Chaucer's. The poet's easy and even inevitable turn from "former" world into the present "("our dayes," continuing into now) is hardly jolting. Literary critics from the early modern period on have often been tempted to view Chaucer as an early exponent of the same later critics' "modern" views. The tossings and turnings of *The Book of the Duchess*, the fitful dreams of Troilus upon his bed, and the refraction of a few estates into uncategorizable individuals on the road to Canterbury all could be read to proclaim Chaucer as a star in self-obsessed modernity's firmament of heroic individuals who have helped to promote the individual's cause. Facing a body of work with such a triumphant sense of character, it's only right to ask how "The Former Age" — anonymously mourning the loss of a community, depicting individuals in the direst terms, and denying any poem to redress the wrongs it tells of — can possibly fit in.

I think that the solution to this puzzle lies in its apparent form: the form not of a polished set of Georgics, still less part of a learned *prosimetrum*, but of a short and affecting, anonymous and vernacular folk song instead. Incongruously bringing to mind the voice of a "folk" in a poem whose classical memory denies folk memory and whose whole purpose seems to be to narrate the loss of such early communal mentality, Chaucer appears to honor that early cohesion ("I" appears nowhere) even while embracing the implications of its loss. Nor are all of these implications necessarily bad in themselves: just as effectively as lack of possessions had, might not a spirit of selfish dissension prevent tyranny from taking root? In that regard Chaucer further suggests that this poem's sense of complaint, or more precisely its welding-together of ambition with complaint, might be able to forge new communities through time if not in space, in the words of polished texts if not in revolution's candid speech.

This essay has suggested that "The Former Age" and its use of a golden age tradition for anonymous lament demonstrates a yearning for production as well as a lack of true feeling in a fallen latter age, the fate of which seems dark indeed. True community in groups, true souls in individuals, seem never to have existed as both we and Chaucer's readers would like to imagine. Human progress appears as dangerous, inexorable and merciless, as the grinding of gears in a machine. Chaucer's "Former Age" is not without its own glimmer of hope, though — an original one at that, precisely through its heavy reliance on the classics and Boethius. No matter his reason for evoking them, *their* former worlds too are made present by his act. That act's power (and their persistence) in themselves have much to teach.

✺ Half Dead
Parsing Cecilia

Nicola Masciandaro

percutis, ut sanes, et occidis nos, ne moriamur abs te
~Augustine, *Confessions*

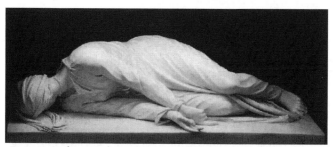

Figure 1. Stefano Maderno (1575-1636), *Martyrdom of Saint Cecilia*,
S. Cecilia in Trastevere, Rome.[1]

§ Synopsis

St. Cecilia's botched beheading in Chaucer's *Second Nun's Tale* masterfully sculpts the conundrum of life/death liminality into a horrific three-day dilation of the moment of martyrdom, opening the decollative blow that typically coincides with receiving its crown into a series of unfinished

---

[1] Photograph by Remi Jouan (2007): http://de.wikipedia.org/wiki/Datei:Santa_Ceciclia_Travesere_statue_%282%29.jpg.

neck-cuts. Pinched between the cruelty of the headsman's impotence, the idiotic inflexibility of the law, and her own sacred durability, Cecilia embodies the paradoxical idea of an unending, asymptotically inconclusive decapitation, an infinite series of beheading blows that never severs the head. Her hacked neck fuses into one form the two principles it figurally evokes: the unbeheadability of the body of God — "illius enim capita membra sumus. Non potest hoc corpus decollari" ["We are limbs of that head. This body cannot be decapitated"][2] — and the semi-living nature of fallen humanity, as signified through medieval allegorical interpretation of the traveler who is attacked by robbers on the road from Jerusalem to Jericho and left "half alive/half dead" [*semivivus, emithane*] (Luke 10:30). The unity of this form is equivalent to the differential non-difference (half alive = half dead) between the Greek and Latin terms. The three-fold opening intensively multiplies the "zero degree of torture"[3] into a single *tertium quid* that is indifferently beyond the distinction between life and death. Being half dead, Cecilia is ultimately alive. Being half alive, Cecilia is ultimately dead. Dwelling in the hyper-intimacy of extreme dereliction, Cecilia is a lacerated, ever-dilating theopathic icon of divinity's absolute indifference to life and death, its being superessentially beyond both. Her three-day rest from both, during which she simultaneously does nothing and works all the more fervently, exemplifies the "passivity and absence of effort . . . in which divine transcendence is dissolved."[4]

> Thre strokes in the nekke he smoot hire tho,
> The tormentour, but for no maner chaunce

---

[2] Augustine, *Ennarationes in Psalmos*, 88.5, in *Patrologia Latina*, ed. J.P. Migne, 217 vols. (Paris, 1844-1855), 37:1122; hereafter referred to as PL, cited by volume and page number.

[3] Michel Foucault, *Discipline and Punish: The Birth of the Prison*, trans. Alan Sheridan (New York: Vintage, 1995), 33.

[4] Georges Bataille, *On Nietzsche*, trans. Bruce Boone (London: Continuum, 2004), 135.

He myghte noght smyte al hir nekke atwo;
And for ther was that tyme an ordinaunce
That no man sholde doon man swich
     penaunce
The ferthe strook to smyten, softe or soore,
This tormentour ne dorste do namoore,
But half deed, with hir nekke ycorven there,
He lefte hir lye, and on his wey he went.
(VIII.526–534)[5]

§ THRE STROKES IN THE NEKKE HE SMOOT HIRE THO

The representation of the three strokes emits several rays of darkness, occult illuminations of significance from what the image hides. First, there is the darkness of the three-ness itself, the obscurity of its relation to the semi-beheading event. That the reason for the three is later provided in no way erases this significant obscurity. Not only does the explanation not touch the question of threeness itself, it rather exacerbates the obscurity by linking three-ness to the arbitrariness of the law, superadding the abstract/bureaucratic violence of law per se to the palpable violence of the strokes and thus intensifying their numerical enigma. This conjunction — an excellent object for contemplating more generally the intimacy between law and number, all the hidden complicities between the law of number and the number of law — is essentially temporal, a repetition of momentary indistinction between the time of the act ("tho") and the time of the law ("ther was that tyme an ordinaunce") that incisionally counts and literally strikes law upon body. (The word *law*, via OE *lagu*, itself indicates something set down, a stroke, and is related to *lecgan* [lay], which also means to slay, strike down; cf. the expression *to lay into* someone). The darkness of this relation, the hidden

---

[5] All citations of Chaucer are from *The Riverside Chaucer*, gen. ed. Larry D. Benson, 3rd edn. (Boston: Houghton Mifflin, 1987), cited by fragment and/or book number, and by line numbers.

mechanical link between the constitutive time of the active instant and the historical time of its situation, opens into the deeper darkness of the triune law of time itself (past, present, future), the inescapability of its numbering. In light of Aristotle's definition of time as "the number of movement in respect of the before and after,"[6] *thre strokes* is simply a *literal intensification of the wound of time*, the continuum of its cutting into being.[7] Still, however deep a significance for the three is given, it never touches the three-ness of the stroke itself as a specific phenomenal reality. For that is something, in its immediate facticity, behind which cause and reason necessarily recede. Three in this sense is the real time of (thinking with) the one experiencing being beheaded, with her who is being capitally cut off from all that does not matter by facing a simple brutality of *one, two, three* — the essential count of ex-per-ience itself or out-through-going. To see this experience (as opposed to imagining what it is *like*) means seeing a *superlative identity* between three and Cecilia's semi-beheading, a direct and immediate identity. This threeness, as the primary, first-word feature of the event, is the threeness of beheading itself, an essential threeness of the act that is paradoxically disclosed, like the being of Heidegger's hammer, when beheading breaks down or fails to fulfill itself. The essential 'count' of beheading is three, in the sense of being a *tertium quid* produced in the severing of the head/body binarism. Compare with: "Severing also is still a joining and relating" and Dante's description of the infernal cephalophore Bertran de Born as "due in uno e uno in due" (*Inferno* 28.125).[8] Beheading unlocks the invisible head-body holism,

---

[6] Aristotle, *Physics*, 220a; in *The Basic Works of Aristotle*, ed. Richard McKeon (New York: Random House, 1941).

[7] The identification of the three strokes with time, as a perfect intersection of *chronos* and *kairos*, passing time and the moment of opportune crisis, is supported by the apocalyptic dimensions of the tale. See Eileen S. Janowski, "Chaucer's 'Second Nun's Tale' and the Apocalyptic Imagination," *Chaucer Review* 36 (2001): 128–148.

[8] "[A]uch das Trennen ist noch ein Verbinden und Beziehen"

the conjunction of each being within the other, into the negative conjunction of severed head *and* body. Decapitation's count is three, and in three distinct ways: 1) *serially*, decapitation is the weird third thing that follows the separation of head (one) from body (two), a neither-head-nor-body that includes and emerges from both; 2) *additively*, decapitation is the sum of its parts: head plus body (head + trunk) equals three, where head must be counted twice, as head and as part of body; 3) *synthetically*, decapitation is three as the union of its dualities, its two-in-one and one-in-two. The three-ness of beheading may also be sought within its twisted temporality, its being a specular folding of past, present, and future, or "an event that ends before it begins and begins after it ends."[9]

Second, there is the darkness of the syntactical contraction of the three strokes into one act. By eliding the experiential space between the strokes, this contraction deepens the event by not dramatizing it, like off-stage violence in a Greek tragedy. *Three strokes in the nekke*, as if part of one design (an idea artistically realized in the Cecilia sculpture at the cathedral in Albi), silently equates the passing of the strokes with the unrepresentable, leaving it suspended and all the more present as something that does not enter into memory. Why? Because the passing of the three strokes, the durational suffering of them, is something radically unworthy of

(Martin Heidegger, "Logik: Heraklits Lehre vom Logos," in *Heraklit*, 'Gesamtausgabe,' Bd. 55 [Frankfurt am Main: Vittorio Klostermann, 1970], 337). Dante Alighieri, *The Divine Comedy*, ed. Giorgio Petrocchi, trans. Charles S. Singleton (Princeton: Princeton University Press, 1979); all further citations of Dante are from this edition, by canto and line number. On these principles, see *And They Were Two In One And One In Two*, eds. Nicola Masciandaro and Eugene Thacker (New York: n.p., 2011).

[9] Nicola Masciandaro, "*Non potest hoc corpus decollari*: Beheading and the Impossible," in *Heads Will Roll: Decapitation in Medieval Literature and Culture*, eds. Larissa Tracy and Jeff Massey (Leiden: E. J. Brill, 2012), 15–39.

recollection. Not because it is to be forgotten, but because it is only *known without recording*, understood immediately in the absence of memorial entrapment and deformation. This silent passing of the strokes does not simply encode trauma, the real live woun*ding* that never passes into language and is (dis)remembered symptomatically. It is something deeper: the exact openness of being wounded that will not, by its own deep transcendence of suffering *in* suffering, be circumscribed in any repetition whatsoever. Behind the baser darkness of the terrifying dilation of decapitation's ideal instantaneity into three-fold time there lies the more brilliant darkness of Cecilia's radical or totally rooted self-opening under the blade, her unrecordable dismembering. The unending opening of beheading into three exposes the shining obscurity of the *deeper time* that is the very place of Cecilia's rootedness in God, the enigmatic ease of her actually being what Gawain only momentarily and with great difficulty achieves: "grathely hit bydez and glent with no membre / Bot stode stylle as the ston other a stubbe auther / That ratheled is in roche grounde with rotez a hundredth" ["Truly he awaits it and flinched with no member, but stood still as a stone, or a stump that is anchored in rocky ground with a hundred roots"].[10] This rootless rootedness or abyssal stillness is the passional seed and prefiguration of the three-day half-death that follows ("Thre dayes lyved she in this torment," VIII.537) — a temporal imitation of Christ's entombment that the triune beheading law enables with perfect providential perversity, intimating a ready-made path to revolutionary salvation via suffering of the law's very letter, i.e., martyrdom as hyper literal head tax: "Render unto Caesar . . ." (Matthew 22:21). The saint's living three days in half-death is not simply the effect of surviving three strokes. It is the fulfillment and produced end of her real passive acting or intentional

---

[10] Anonymous, *Gawain and the Green Knight*, in *Poems of the Pearl Manuscript*, eds. Malcolm Andrew and Ronald Waldron (Berkeley: University of California Press, 1978), ll. 2293–2295.

endurance of all of them as one. Without this mysterious intention the specific duration of the survival would be senseless, whence Cecilia's subsequent revelation of her secret request, *To han respite thre dayes and namo* (VIII.543), and its correspondence with the three-stroke maximum: *This tormentour ne dorste do namoore* (VIII.532). Note also the formulation of the wish, as if the prolonging of her death were a postponement of, or even rest from, execution (*respite* also connotes cessation of suffering),[11] rather than its brutally extended form. Occupying the negativity of limit (*namoore*), the full threshold of the end, Cecilia here demonstrates how transcendent ceaselessness is a constraint-based art, a spiritual exercise of freedom that necessarily and paradoxically operates within strict conditions. Never ceasing — *She nevere cessed* (VIII.124); *nevere cessed* (VIII.538) — is an infinite work of finitude, not a task of those who think they have all day. The darkness of Cecilia's intense openness to beheading may thus be formulated as an aggressive form of *amor fati* that fiercely insists from within on experiencing all three strokes, on passing through the full force of necessity, precisely without recourse to any external means that would enforce or facilitate that passage. The prolongation it produces is not a matter of experience-hunger, of wanting more life. Rather it is the need to arrive oneself to the real end, as opposed to merely being there when it is over. The last thing a saint wants is to die in her sleep. Die awake, so awake that experience runs ahead of death; show up for life, *finally*. Cecilia is not loitering or lingering on the boundary between this life and the next — "surely it is the height of folly for you to linger on this bridge."[12] She is crossing it so busily that death itself cannot happen or take place without protracted difficulty. In sum, the real subject of *Thre strokes in the nekke . . .* is the preposition *in*, the place where Cecilia's desire

---

[11] *Middle English Dictionary*, *s.v.* "respite," 1b.

[12] Hakim Sinai, *The Walled Garden of Truth*, trans. David Pendlebury (London: Octagon Press, 1974), 52.

operates, freely exposing the strength of its utter submission to God. Julian of Norwich understands this: "I harde telle . . . of the storye of Sainte Cecille . . . that she hadde thre woundes with a swerde in the nekke . . . By the stirringe of this, I consyvede a mighty desire, pryande oure lorde God that he wolde graunte me thre woundes in my life time [contrition, compassion, and longing for God] . . . *withouten any condition*."[13] As does Bataille: "incapable of doing anything — I survive — in laceration. And with my eyes, I follow a shimmering light that turns me into its plaything."[14]

Third, there is the darkness of the headsman's intention. The primary and normal sense is that the headsman is not intending three strokes but is attempting thrice to behead her in one. This is supported by the assumption that this is what he, as headsman, should be intending and by the subsequent indication that was unable to (*He myghte noght*), which implies that he was in fact trying his best or attempting to apply a maximum of strength and skill to the effort. This is also supported by the earliest version of the *Passio* and subsequent versions: "[Q]uam cum speculator tertio ictu percussisset, caput eius amputare non potuit";[15] "Quam spiculator tribus ictibus in collo percussit, sed tamen caput eius amptare non potuit";[16] "The quellar smot with al his mayn, threo sithe on the swere / He ne mighte for nothinge smitten hit of."[17] Yet there are other more obscure possibilities, various clouds in the headsman's will, divisible into those that fall under the normal sense of his intention and those that do not. The former will be more properly

---

[13] *The Writings of Julian of Norwich*, eds. Nicholas Watson & Jacqueline Jenkins (University Park: Pennsylvania State University Press, 2006), 65, my emphasis.

[14] *On Nietzsche*, trans. Bruce Boone (London: Continuum, 1992), 91.

[15] Giacomo Laderchi, *S. Caeciliae Virg[inis] et Mart[yris] Acta. . .* (Rome, 1723), 38.

[16] Jacobus de Voragine, *Legenda Aurea*, ed. T. Graesse (Leipzig: Impensis Librariae Arnoldianae, 1850), 777.

[17] *The Life of St. Cecilia*, ed. Albert S. Cook (Boston, 1898), 91.

discussed with respect to the next line. The latter comprises several intersecting possibilities, all of which are supported by the basely literal sense of *Thre strokes . . . he smoot hire*, namely, that the headsman simply struck Cecilia three times in the neck. Some of these are: 1) that the headsman wanted to torture Cecilia, to deny her a quick death, either by protracting the beheading or not beheading her at all; 2) that he did not want to harm Cecilia, but was compelled to, and thus did so minimally; 3) that he didn't care about what he was doing and performed the task without proper intention; and 4) that he was intentionally conflicted, subject to opposed desires, and acted through some complicated combination of the above, perhaps changing his mind in the process. There is also a third and stranger kind of intentional darkness that is between and outside these distinctions, namely, the possibility that the headsman did indeed try his best but only via a pure and spontaneous decay of intention, a nameless form of volitional perforation whereby the will, not in relation to any other interfering object but precisely in relation to nothing, secretly and suddenly (*sua sponte*), lacks itself. Such intention is dark in the sense of being the subject of a *clinamen* or weird swerve that occurs, as Lucretius says, at no fixed place or time, only here the *clinamen* must be construed as itself weirded by the full perseveration of the originary intention — a swerve that travels in a straight line, as it were. Such a dark will, a will that purely is and is not one's own, is well figured in the three non-severing strokes in that they do hit their mark, but inexplicably without realization of the intention for doing so. Although this potential negative spontaneity of the headsman's will must be thought apart from possibilistic conditions or chance, it may be inversely compared to the event and experience of hitting a target by only diffidently or naively attempting to, that is, the situation where one succeeds in fulfilling an intention without *really* trying to. In that case, an intention's deficiency becomes the paradoxical means of its realization, so that one strangely *cannot take credit for succeeding at what one meant to do*. In this case, an intention's integrity is the paradoxical site of its non-realization (but not because of any external factors), so that one must take credit (if that were possible) for failing at what one meant to do *on the basis of that meaning alone*, that is, for a pure, unknowable, and thus unconfessable kind of failure that cannot properly be located in the will, or its application, or the difference between them. Although this third kind of intentional darkness is very difficult to conceive in practical terms, it may be fittingly defined in this hagiographic context as a *momentary negative occasionalism* or local withdrawal of divine omnipresence as universal intermediary of all action. The idea of such withdrawal also furnishes a more general theory of passion miracles, which so often involve a suspension of the capacity for things to touch, especially in the context of the comic impotence of violence to effect its ends. This may be conceived externally (blades fail to cut, fire fails to burn, etc.) but also internally, with respect to the mechanics of mental powers, so that the headsman's will may be thought of as failing to touch itself and thus spinning in place like a disengaged *primum mobile*. The will still moves, gives every appearance of being itself, yet is somehow suspended in an essential detachment from its own being. Such a darkening of the headsman's will, which may be correlated as well to the executioner's traditional head covering and its symbolic removal of personal agency from legal murder, thus represents the perfect profane counterpoint to the celestial motion of Cecilia: "[As] hevene is swift and round and eek brennynge, / Right so was faire Cecilie the white / Ful swift and bisy evere in good werkynge, / And round and hool in good perseverynge / And brennynge evere in charite ful brighte" (VIII.114–118). Ultimately, the dark will of the headsman is visible as the intimate shadow of Cecilia's own, the adjacent negative outline of her alchemical burning and melting into God.

§ He myghte noght smyte al hir nekke atwo

The headsman's failure to sever Cecilia's neck, considered as an eventual contradiction or prevention of his exercised will, fulfills the characteristically Christian renunciatory logic of strength-through-weakness: "for when I am weak, then I am strong" (2 Corinthians 12:10). There is a real dialectical relation between Cecilia's self-exposure and her material power to withstand the tormentor's blows. The obscurity of this relation concerns the actual location of this strength, which may be understood as existing everywhere, nowhere, or locally somewhere. Of these possibilities, locating the power in her neck seems the simplest and most physically plausible solution. It also offers the beauty of an inverse re-writing of the biblical trope of "stiff-necked" (*durae cervicis*) pride (e.g. Exodus 34:9, compare with "la cervice mia superba," Dante, *Purgatorio* 11.53), whereby the humble neck, bending itself freely before the blow, achieves a truly superior durability. Literalizing in reverse the psychomachean allegory of Humility's decapitation of Pride,[18] Cecilia's humbly-strong cervix stops the instrument that would violate it, exposing the fundamental weakness of its wielder vis-à-vis her uncuttable sancity — a correlative fulfillment of the verse, "Dominus iustus concidit cervices peccatorum" ["The Lord who is just will cut the necks of sinners"] (Psalms 128.4). As this line is read by Augustine in reference to "proud sinners in particular, the arrogant, stiff-necked kind,"[19] so Cecilia's saintly neck-strength signifies an ordinate spiritual obstinacy and pride, a pure relentless refusal of the false which is paradoxically demonstrated in the inviolable openness and impenetrable nudity of an extreme passivity that renders action itself passive and inoperative, making agency the comically abject

---

[18] See text of poem in Prudentius, *Against Symmachus*, ed. H.J. Thomson, Vol. 2 (Cambridge, Mass.: Loeb Classical Library, 1979), 109–143 (esp. ll. 280–286).

[19] Augustine, *Expositions of the Psalms*, trans. Maria Boulding (Hyde Park: New City Press, 2004), 128.4.

subject of its patient. On this point the impotent headsman is unveiled as the profane opposite of Cecilia's angelic protector, who will instantly kill whoever improperly touches her body: "I have an aungel which that loveth me, / That with greet love, wher so I wake or sleepe, / Is redy ay my body for to kepe. / And if that he may feelen, out of drede, / That ye me touche, or love in vileynye, / He right anon wol sle yow with the dede" (VIII.152–157). In light of this aura of protection, it is all the more meaningful, as an image of authentic or do-it-yourself sanctity, that Cecilia appears to survive beheading on her own strength, without external intervention of the sort provided by John the Baptist when Sanctulus of Nursia, facing the power of "the strongest headsman, of whom there was no doubt that with one stroke he could sever the head," calls out, "Saint John, get hold of him!" and "instantly the striker's arm became stiff and inflexible, and held the sword heavenward."[20] Still, the precise nature of the *no maner chaunce* whereby the executioner *myghte not* sever Cecilia's neck remains uncertain. The expression *no maner chaunce* signifies impossibility as a negativity or limit that governs probability from the outside and also suggests the idea of proving that impossibility through exhaustion of possibilities, the failure of trial and error. This sense fulfills the weaker sense of *myghte*, "in which the ability or potentiality becomes mere possibility,"[21] whereas the stronger sense (to be strong, have power, be able) makes less sense when governed by *no maner chaunce.*[22] Indeed, the semantic hierarchy of the verb provides

[20] Jacobus de Voragine, *The Golden Legend*, trans. William Granger Ryan, 2 vols. (Princeton: Princeton University Press, 1993), 2:140.

[21] *Middle English Dictionary*, *s.v.* "mouen," 3.

[22] More generally, the text requires us to undecidably entertain the differences between: a) the headsman in no way having sufficient power to sever Cecilia's neck (because it is too resilient, naturally or supernaturally); b) the headsman's having sufficient power to sever her neck and in no way being able to activate it for some reason; and c) the headsman's having sufficient power and activating it but in no way succeeding to sever her neck because of some contingency.

a good account, whatever the specific actuality of the event, of the swordsman's situation as a suffering of the demotion of one's power into an unavailable option, the becoming impossible of a power. The causal darkness of the scene thus lies precisely in its representation of an odd event of obstacleless interruption: nothing interferingly *stops* you from doing what you are doing but something nonetheless prevents it from *happening*. The negative or non-event reaches reversely into new and seemingly impossible forms of impossibility, all the stranger because things *are* working, moving forward, namely, the sword is indeed cutting into Cecilia's flesh. The wonder of the semi-beheading revolves around a pair of unaccountable intersecting conjunctions: the executioner's simultaneous impotency and effectivity, and the saint's simultaneous durability and receptivity. To synthesize these double sides of the situation is difficult. Moving in the direction of diffuseness, we may imagine deficient blows slicing into minimally resistant flesh, a kind of pathetic miraculous in which the divine power can only barely raise itself into the world by displacing a little of the world's own force, sucking a small amount of power from the agent and blowing it into the patient. Moving in the direction of intensity, we may imagine very powerful blows slicing maximally resistant flesh, a kind of heroic miraculous in which the divine power cannot resist dramatically presenting itself by meeting the force of the world face to face, inspiring the patient with power to endure an equally inspired agent. Alternately, we may imagine some admixture of the two alternatives spread across the three strokes, or a mutual cancellation of them altogether: a truly ridiculous eventuality in which the saint requires no divine intervention whatsoever because her neck is naturally strong enough to survive three blows from an inept headsman. All possibilities violate the

---

Inability must be distinguished from impossibility, even though they may overlap. Aristotle considers the senses of inability as privation of potency in *Metaphysics*, 1046a (*Basic Works of Aristotle*).

decollative ideal of instantaneous death and thereby only exacerbate the spectacle of suffering, multiplying the three blows into a matrix of possibilities that nowhere presents any relief from their endurance. Nor is the darkness of the situation's causal insolubility ever resolved. Rather, it is marvelously all-the-more occluded by the raw presence of Cecilia's suffering and the subsequent revelation of her wish, in which the weird *how* of the event is transmuted into the fulfillment of its demonstrative actuality: "Thre dayes lyved she in this torment . . . 'I axed this of hevene kyng'" (VIII.537–542). And yet the specificity of the request and its fulfillment only underscores the realization of a precise modulation of psycho-physical forces that ends life in three days through wounds. Volitionally persevering herself as an unseverable unicity that *will not* be cut "atwo," Cecilia chooses, with more or less understanding of that will's operation, even the terms of her affliction.[23]

§ HALF DEED

The term *half deed* correctly translates *seminecem* from the original *Passio*: "seminecem eam cruentus carnifex dereliquit" (38). In the *Legenda Aurea*, which Chaucer also drew upon,

---

[23] My argument thus fulfills, by taking one step further, Elizabeth Robertson's reading of Chaucer's Cecilia as an exemplar of the "inherently radical nature" of choice ("Apprehending the Divine and Choosing to Believe: Voluntarist Free Will in Chaucer's *Second Nun's Tale*," *The Chaucer Review* 46 [2011]: 130). Robertson emphasizes "Cecilia's choice to exert her free will . . . despite extreme physical exertion" (129) and more importantly, discerns how violence in the tale is "a metaphor for the nature of choice itself" in light of the voluntarist understanding of choice as marking "a radical shift from one domain to the next, from indeterminacy to determinacy, from potency to act" (130). My point is that precisely in these terms Cecilia's will must be read as mysteriously touching and operating upon the reality of her own execution.

semivivam sometimes occurs.[24] The interchangeability of the terms is indicated by an entry in the *Medulla Grammatice*: "Seminecis: half dede, half kwyk,"[25] but similar attention to literal correctness is shown in the two versions of the Wycliffite Bible, which translate the half-alive victim of the good Samaritan parable ("et plagis impositis abierunt semivivo relicto," Luke 10:30) with "half quyk" and "half alyue,"[26] and in Langland's version of the parable we have: "for semyvif he semed, / And as naked as a needle, and noon help abouten."[27] *Half-dead* may enjoy a certain general conceptual priority over *half-alive*, insofar as the term is deployed by the living, from the perspective of life, within which it seems more natural to think the liminal state in terms of the constitutive opposite (death) rather than the pure privation of one's own state. The distinction between the interchangeable terms is also clearly related to the *connoted futurity of emphasis*, where the chosen term implies a potential for or movement into its increase, i.e., *half-alive* as nearly dead and (perhaps) going-to-live, *half-dead* as barely alive and (perhaps) going-to-die. The distinction was in fact important to medieval exegesis of good Samaritan parable, for which *half-alive* signifies the fallen but redeemable nature of sinful humanity,[28] as clarified in the twelfth-century *Lambeth Homilies*:

> They (the devils) left him half alive; half alive he was when that he had sorrow within himself for his sins.

---

[24] Sherry L. Reames, "The Second Nun's Prologue and Tale," in *Sources and Analogues of the Canterbury Tales I*, eds. Robert M. Correale and Mary Hamel, 2 vols. (Cambridge, Eng.: D.S. Brewer, 2002), 1:514.

[25] *Middle English Dictionary, s.v.* "half," adj. 1c.

[26] *Middle English Dictionary, s.v.* "half," adj. 1c.

[27] *The Vision of Piers Plowman: A Complete Edition of the B-Text*, ed. A.V.C. Schmidt (London: J. M. Dent & Sons, 1978), B.XVII.57–58.

[28] See, for example, Origen, *Homilies on Luke*, trans. Joseph T. Lienhard (Washington, DC: Catholic University of America Press, 1996), Homily 34; Augustine, *Sermo* 131.6; PL 38:732.

> Here we ought to understand why it says 'half alive'
> [*alf quic*] and not 'half dead'. Hereof we may take an
> example by two brands (torches), when the one is
> aquenched altogether, and the other is aquenched
> except a little spark; the one that hath the one spark in
> it we may blow and it will quicken (revive) and kindle
> the whole brand. The brand that is wholly quenched,
> though one blow on it for ever, may never again be
> kindled. These two brands betoken two men: the one
> sinneth and is sorry for his sin, but cannot subdue his
> flesh . . . This other man sinneth and loveth his sins.[29]

In light of the half-alive/half-dead distinction, there are
several specific senses to Chaucer's use of *half deed* in relation
to Cecilia. First, *half deed* emphasizes the fact that she is going
to die, that she is closer to death than life, yet precisely for that
reason nonetheless alive and indeed paradoxically living all
the more intensely in intimacy with the other side of life for
the three days during which she "never cessed hem the faith to
teche / That she hadde fostred" (VIII.538–539). Second, the
term emphasizes, in light of the allegorical logic of the
Samaritan parable, Cecilia's independence from external
divine aid, the fact that her martyric miracle consists only in a
little more life. That is all she requires. No supernatural
displays, no hagio-grotesque cephalophory, no dramatic leap
into the *al di là*, just a three-day expansion of the "zero degree
of torture" into an opportunity "that I myghte do werche"
(VIII.545). Rather than a liberating spiritual consummation of
the sort exemplified by Prudentius's account of St. Agnes's
beheading, in which angelic flight follows a swift death,[30]

---

[29] *Old English Homilies and Homiletic Treatises*, ed. Richard Morris
(London: N. Trubner & Co., 1868), 80.

[30] "[S]he bowed her head and humbly worshipped Christ, so that her
bending neck should be readier to suffer the impending blow; and
the executioner's hand fulfilled her great hope, for at one stroke he
cut off her head and swift death forestalled the sense of pain. Now
the disembodied spirit springs forth and leaps in freedom into the

Cecilia's passion fulfills itself in her staying here, in remaining, lying in the state in which the world leaves her. Third, *half deed* harmonizes with the principle of *mors mystica*, the mystic death to self necessary for divine union, as per Julian of Norwich's "mighty desire" for an unconditional spiritual wounding cited above. It places the saint, still living, wholly *within* death, disclosing at once the saint's self-transcendence and the fundamental unreality of death itself. Here *half deed* perfectly signifies the essential negativity of the realization of a pure, as it were, contentless plenitude, like the *actus purus* identified with God, in which experience, the whole out-through-going of temporal being, is abandoned in the very midst of time, "not an experience of absence but rather an absence of experience — or even better, a point of indiscretion where this distinction would itself collapse."[31] Fourth, *half deed* partakes of Chaucer's characteristic death-privileging interest in figuring life/death liminality: "neither quyk ne ded" (*Troilus and Criseyde* 3.79); "Always deynge and be not ded" (*Book of the Duchess* 588), "Myself I mordre with my privy thought" (*Anelida and Arcite* 291); "My throte is kut unto my nekke boon . . . and as by wey of kynde / I sholde have dyed, ye, longe tyme agon" (*Prioress's Tale* VII.649–651); "and leften hire for deed, and wenten away" (*Tale of Melibee* VII.972), etc. This interest is most clearly shown in his handling of the scene of Arcite and Palamon's discovery in the *Knight's Tale*. Boccaccio, his source, places great emphasis on the vital sensitivity of the wounded knights, who cry out when they are found: "due giovani fediti dolorando / quivi trovaro, sanz' alcun riposo; / e ciaschedun la morte domandava, / tanto dolor del lor mal gli gravava" ["they found there two young men critically wounded and in constant pain; and so much did the pain of their injuries afflict them, that each one begged

---

air, and angels are around her as she passes along the shining path" (Prudentius, *Crowns of Martyrdom*, in Prudentius, *Against Symmachus,* 14.85–93).

[31] Thomas A. Carlson, *Indiscretion: Finitude and the Naming of God* (Chicago: University of Chicago Press, 1999), 257.

to die"].[32] Chaucer elides completely this pain and passion, replacing it with a double negative that pushes their being into a more purely liminal state of suspension: "Nat fully quyke, ne fully dede they were" (I.1015). Subtracted from both life and death, the double knights appropriately inhabit a strange kind of vaguely intensive double death, half-dead to life and half-dead to death, which produces a dark suggestion proper to the tale: they may be brought back to life, but only for further death. The scene provides a clarifying counterpoint to Cecilia's passion. Where the Theban knights' neither-live-nor-dead state represents a passive death-in-life that may be awakened to deathly passion, Cecilia's half-death embodies an active life-in-death that expresses and opens into supra-living passion, "brennyge ever in charite ful brighte" (*Knight's Tale* VIII.118), i.e. the superessential divine life that "live[s] in a fashion surpassing other living things."[33] Crucially, however, Chaucer places the superlative intensity of Cecilia's saintly living wholly within *this* life, without any reference to another world or afterlife, and thus necessarily within death—an orientation that participates in the tale's emphasis on the availability of paradise in the temporal here and now: "The swete smel that in myn herte I fynde / Hath chaunged me al in another kynde" (VIII.251–252). There is another world: this one. Cecilia's half-death is deathly, ghastly, an 'unbearable' torment of being neither here nor there, alive nor dead. Yet it is so precisely as an index of the general lived nature of this life vis-à-vis its radical potential to produce and experience the true *anagogy of the present*, a foretaste of eternity that needs no future or other life. Next to this revolutionary life, the whole world is indeed half-dead.

---

[32] Boccaccio, *Teseida* 2.85; cited from Robert M. Correale and Mary Hamel, *Sources and Analogues of the Canterbury Tales*, 2 vols. (Cambridge: D.S. Brewer, 2003), 2:138.

[33] Pseudo-Dionysius, *Divine Names*, 5.3; in *Complete Works*, trans. Colm Luibheid (New York: Paulist Press, 1987).

§ HE LEFTE HIR LYE, AND ON HIS WEY HE WENT

The executioner's abandonment of Cecilia, especially with the reference to "his wey," which is nowhere in the sources, evokes the dereliction of the victim in the good Samaritan parable, left "half-alive" on the road between Jerusalem and Jericho. In this context, the executioner emerges more specifically as a liminal figure intentionally half way between the thieves who harm the victim and the travelers who fail to help him. He is like the thieves in that he is the direct agent of the violence and a willing participant in its purpose. He is like the passersby in that he is not himself the cause of the violence, but someone who similarly fails to help the victim, neither caring for her nor mercifully killing her. In these terms he is a special kind of subject of the law, the subject who enforces its letter but remains neutral with respect to the present, situational question of its spirit, someone seemingly equally unable/unwilling to either stand outside the law (do anything beyond it) or transgress it (do anything against it). The tormentor's walking away is a conspicuous index of this inability/unwillingness, an a-instrumental surplus action that also marks him as a subject in the first place, an individualized intentional being who exists in relation to things whether he will or no. Crucially, the action encompasses opposite possibilities, possibilities which indeterminately coincide around the specificity of "his way," that is, around the indication that the tormentor does not simply walk away, but takes a way specific to him. On the one hand, the tormentor's walking away suggests the idea of open refusal, not in the name of anything, but simply in the name of what is other than the situation at hand. On the other hand, the walking away suggests not refusal at all, but only a movement into nothing, or the movement of whatever kind of self-interest, having 'something better' to do. There is no deciding the intention of the tormentor's walking way—that is the point. He appears only in his disappearance and through a fundamental ambivalence, at once a potentially redeemable subject of the drama, an outsider with a future perhaps intimately related to its truth, and its worst kind of protagonist, a pure practitioner of its (ideological) structure, the truly neither-living-nor-dead, neither-hot-nor-cold subject whose business-as-usual, spiritless 'life' is nothing but a self-serving and sleepily sinful concatentation of omissive com-missions and comissive omissions.

Chaucer's interest in the figure of the executioner as subject is also indicated by his non-translation of the vilifying, objectifying adjectives applied to him in the sources (*cruentus*, *truculentus*). Instead, the poet gives him no adjectives at all and signifies him deictically, "This tormentor," which has the effect of identifying him as a specific person, an individual: This dark *who* is neither a character nor a mere human prop, but someone whose intentionality is essentially and con-stitutively bound up with the climactic event of the drama, but in a fundamentally impersonal way. As my analysis has hopefully shown, Cecilia's near beheading is unthinkable without reference to what is 'going on' with the headsman, what is up with him. His failure to finish the job is not only negatively at the center of the show, but is ironically upstaged by the saint's dynamic ability to complete her work three days beyond the evident hour of her death. It signifies both as a negative exemplum of the work-ethic that governs the tale and as an indispensable cog in the providential logic of the hagiography. What accounts for Chaucer's creation of this indeterminate space of identity around Cecilia's tormentor?

Nothing, I prefer to think. Allowing the headsman to walk away and be his own no-one, Chaucer exercises a dark, inscrutable charity toward the even darker subject of the spiritless law.

In the Event of the *Franklin's Tale*

J. Allan Mitchell

There is no truth to delimit in the event. Events come, if ever they arrive, to designate fields of pure possibility and emergent futurity. Consider one old tale of "diverse aventures" (V.710), Chaucer's *Franklin's Tale*.[1] Somewhere in Brittany, Dorigen is happily married to the knight Arveragus, having recently pledged her undying love. "Have heer my trouthe — til that myn herte breste" (V.759). Soon he goes on an expedition abroad. Dorigen watches ships come to port in the hopes that one will return her husband safely, and she is tormented by thoughts of his foundering. Dorigen cultivates a "derke fantasye" (V.844), meditating on the hazards of a seascape that consists of "grisly rokkes blake" (V.859) just offshore. They are menacing and apparently meaningless obstacles to her happiness. She cannot shake bleak thoughts of a possible fatality, despite friends' comforting words and pleasant distractions. Then something unexpected does happen. At a dance, the amorous squire Aurelius propositions Dorigen, begging her mercy. She rejects his advances, tactfully couching her reply in terms that are described as playful: she says she will yield to Aurelius only if he removes the dangerous rocks that threaten her beloved husband. "Have heer my trouthe, in al that evere I kan" (V.998). It would seem

---

[1] All citations of Chaucer's *Franklin's Tale* are from *The Riverside Chaucer*, gen. ed. Larry D. Benson, 3rd edn. (Boston: Houghton Mifflin, 1987), by fragment and line number.

impossible. But Dorigen's so-called rash promise to Aurelius is a fateful utterance carried away by further events, accompanied by a powerful sense of foreboding, setting in motion so many impossibilities. Dorigen and expectant readers of the tale subsequently drift towards a future of still more improbable events.

The *Franklin's Tale* is a tale of real "aventure," the ramifications of which are hard to fathom. Radical contingency acts as a solvent to sense and significance for anyone who begins to contemplate all of the reversals of fortune. Prodigal in the extreme, the tale can seem almost gratuitous, aleatory, free-wheeling. It is notable that Chaucer generates the crisis for characters and readers alike from within a quasi-pagan perspective that shows little respect for Christian theodicy, imagining a remote time and place — a heathen Breton outcrop before the arrival of the Truth — where there is no assurances of providential rule, reason, or justice. Neither does the tale issue an ultimate truth about the events it describes: the narrative is strictly a-theistic insofar as events are refractory to creeds, themes, and theses, though even that may be affirming too much. Here whatever meaning is arrived at, the truth is another eventuality. But you get the drift.

§ BECOMING *ASTONED*

As indicated, Dorigen makes confident professions of her "trouthe" on two occasions, and then gets carried away. But you could hardly have expected more from her in the event. Notice how she takes the "grisly rokkes blake" to be unyielding fixtures. They will underwrite her truth, projecting her into unknown futures:

> Eterne God, that thurgh thy purveiaunce
> Ledest the world by certein governaunce,
> In ydel, as men seyn, ye no thyng make.
> But, Lord, thise grisly feendly rokkes blake,
> That semen rather a foul confusion

Of werk than any fair creacion
Of swich a parfit wys God and a stable,
Why han ye wroght this werk unresonable?
For by this werk, south, north, ne west, ne eest,
Ther nys yfostred man, ne bryd, ne beest;
It dooth no good, to my wit, but anoyeth.
Se ye nat, Lord, how mankynde it destroyeth?
An hundred thousand bodyes of mankynde
Han rokkes slayn, al be they nat in mynde . . .
(V.865–878)

She sees no rapprochement between the articles of faith (divine *purveiaunce* and *governaunce*) and material conditions on the ground, pitting one against the other. Both seem inexorable. The rocks for their part evoke the terror of hard and intractable reality set against other things relatively soft and vulnerable to change, namely those "hundred thousand bodyes of mankynde." The evidence points to "foul confusion," not "fair creacion," though she imagines some clever clerk might nonetheless lamely argue, "al is for the beste" (V.886). But none steps forward, and Dorigen dilates on the damned confusion, as if taking up a theologian's task. The situation is darker and more demanding than it first appears, and it implicates readers who follow and feel for her plight. It is basically the ignorance you share with Dorigin, locked into resonance with her sense of the occasion. Characters and readers both reside in the exigent moment of particular narrative occurrence into which vital bodies are thrown, prior to the realization of any authorial order (*purveiaunce* and *governaunce* again), where you wrestle with things as a set of eventualities, fortuities, flukes. The threat seems to lie in the stability and solidity of the rocks, but of course no one ever expects the worst. How could Dorigen anticipate the event? Could you?

For the time being the black rocks seem to guarantee her stability no matter what may occur, grounding her assertion of "trouthe." That becomes clear in her promise to Aurelius:

> Looke what day that endelong Britayne
> Ye remoeve alle the rokkes, stoon by stoon,
> That they ne lette ship ne boot to goon —
> I seye, whan ye han maad the coost so clene
> Of rokkes that ther nys no stoon ysene,
> Thanne wol I love yow best of any man;
> Have heer my trouthe, in al that evere I kan.
> (V.992–998)

She plainly means what she says, "in pley" (V.988): she in effect asserts that when lovers can remodel coastlines at will, only then would she betray her marriage vows, for the known world would have become so unnatural and untrue that there would be no grounds for constancy. And that if the rocks were removed, she would have cleared the way for her husband's safe landing, which only then could make a sacrifice of her constancy tolerable. This is facetious hyperbole, but it is near the truth. Far from giving in to adulterous desire, she expresses heartfelt concern for her husband Arveragus. Aurelius immediately grasps the import: "'Madame,' quod he, 'this were an inpossible!'" (V.1009).

Both assume that things will remain the same, and yet Dorigen's playful promise will betray her when circumstances change so drastically as to reorder her understanding of truth, freedom, possibility, and substance. Anything is possible in the event. As it happens, she encounters the actual fluidity of the coastline when the rocks *are* made to disappear into the shoals. Not just the content of her words but also the foundation of the world becomes liquid, labile, groundless. It turns out that Aurelius has employed a canny clerk from Orleans to help remove all the rocks, stone by stone. Capable of clever illusions and "magyk natureel" (V.1125, 1155), the clerk somehow manages to make them disappear for a week or two. For Dorigen the event is distressing, and completely unexpected. A familiar waterfront view has in effect regressed to the primordial moment of flux at creation — as when the earth was void and empty, and darkness was upon the face of the deep, and the spirit of god moved over the waters – the shore having been reconstituted as the site of pure potentiality. The scene is aqueous chaos. It is all a revelation to Dorigen — as it must be to the reader, since to this day no adequate explanation has yet been found for it. She says:

> "Alas," quod she, "that evere this sholde happe!
> For wende I nevere by possibiltee
> That swich a monstre or merveille myghte be!
> It is agayns the process of nature." (V.1342–1345)

Would it have helped to recall that stone, as medieval science taught, is made up of quantities of earth and water? What about the proverbial rock worn away by drops of water? The lithic is not opposed to the liquid in any event, but constitutes one of the natural forms it takes. Rocks decompose and deliquesce, ever morphing, as an acquaintance with Albertus Magnus's *Book of Minerals* could have revealed. And yet Dorigen meets with something of a different order of magnitude, events "agayns the process of nature." She is the victim of another science ("magyk natureel") and untold "possibilitee." There is no adequate explanation. The difficulty now is in coming to see rocks *as* events, or soft bodies just as vulnerable to tides of change. The shocking mutability of these things represents the terror of a fluid reality.

Dorigen suffers from an unexpected sea change, and readers are similarly situated. It is a traumatic occurrence thick with implication for the reified subject and object, where personal identity appears to ebb and flow with the natural environment. Things are rendered coalescent in a manner that can seem almost fated, foregone — but which only now are gathered in a singular, unexpected happenstance ("happe"). You start to make the connections after the fact. First, before anything much had happened, Dorigen was figured as a petroglyph impressed by the consolatory words of her friends: "By process, as ye knowen everichoon, / Men may so longe graven in a stoon, / Til som figure therinne emprented be" (V.829–831). The analogy is as prescient as her very name, Dorigen evoking *Droguen,* a prominent rock along the coast of Penmarch where she settles with her husband in Brittany.[2] Subsequently, the rocks having vanished by some inscrutable magical means, Dorigin becomes "astoned" (V.1339), petrified. Then she contemplates disappearing, considering a suicide that would have her dissolve into some earthy or oceanic substrate, returning to the elements. So her body is at once figured as a hardened substitute in the face of chaos (as if mineralizing to compensate for the absence of the rocks) and a recapitulation (threatening to dematerialize and deliquesce), but in either case she becomes newly incorporated and environed. Who knew the possibilities of stone, sea, desire, language?

What makes her situation so astonishing is the combination of groundlessness and the thrilling freedom it represents — that is, the freedom for matters to be otherwise "by possibilitee." Dorigen becomes one changed thing among others in the world, nothing so self-sufficient or self-evident as she had imagined. The realization is probably not so liberating for her as it is for Aurelius, who has now removed the obstacles to his desire. Dorigen's husband has safely returned from overseas by this point in the tale, but no matter: Aurelius expects her to keep her promise. She contemplates suicide to escape the catastrophe. "'Allas,' quod she, 'on thee, Fortune, I pleyne, / That unwar wrapped hast me in thy cheyne'" (V.1355–1356). She has dodged one horrible eventuality (the death of her husband) only to be faced with another (the impending betrayal of her husband). Owing to a strange fortuity, she seems least capable of changing her circumstances. And yet they will *again.*

§ NARRATIVE *AVENTURE*

The event is a litho-literary phenomenon, pertaining to things

---

[2] John S. P. Tatlock, *The Scene of the Franklin's Tale Visited* (London: Kegan Paul, Trench, Trübner and Co., 1914), 37–40.

as real as stones and the words used to depict them after the fact, inasmuch as both emerge as incipiencies and possibilities. It is perhaps the literary situation *par excellence.* For the careful reader will experience a profound sort of disorientation, consisting of an irruption of pure potentiality into the present without any determinate future direction. Everything is in a state of emergency, and nothing can simply be "read off" a given world. Only by going on, selecting out one actual occurrence from all the possible ones, do things take shape in this strange tale.[3] In the event, Dorigen reveals her plight to her husband, and he wishes her to keep her truth despite all the changes that have brought her to the current impasse: "Ye shul youre trouthe holden, by my fay! / . . . Trouthe is the hyeste thyng that man may kepe" (V.1474, 1479). It is an unexpected concession, and you are invited to interpret.

Indeed it is precisely at this juncture that the focus comes to rest on that construal: you are asked to make a decision. Circumstances spill over — triggering an emergency not just for the fictional characters involved in the story but also for anyone caught up in the narration. Pausing a little, the Franklin addresses the audience's incredulity towards the events narrated thus far:

> Paraventure an heep of yow, ywis,
> Wol holden hym [Arveragus] a lewed man in this
> That he wol putte his wyf [Dorigen] in jupartie.
> Herkeneth the tale er ye upon hire crie.
> She may have bettre fortune than yow semeth;
> And whan that ye han herd the tale, demeth.
> (V.1493–1498)

---

[3] As Jill Mann says in *Feminizing Chaucer* (Cambridge, Eng.: Cambridge University Press, 2002), the tale "embraces the potentiality of Dorigen's rape, of her suicide, of the life-long stain on marital happiness, as it embraces the possibility of Arveragus's shipwreck, or Dorigen's betrayal" (95).

References to fortune and futurity multiply here and elsewhere in the tale (*paraventure, jupartie, fortune*), driving home the point — it is a tale in which anything can happen. There is a chance that the literary matter may be as lithic (meaning quite labile and liquid, as we now see) as the coastal terrain that was made to disappear so suddenly. You can hardly be complacent about present crisis. At this critical moment, you are implicated in an ethical decision about whether to go on. Action ceases, suspended between who-knows-what futures. The Franklin addresses the reader, and you must decide to stop or forbear the consequences. Should you arrest the narrative flow and render judgment now? An audience may "deme" well enough: Arveragus now seems complicit in Dorigen's ruin. But the tale simultaneously pulls in another direction, holding out a possibility — if not the likelihood — of some "bettre fortune." Is that not the main drift? The Franklin for his part, an occasional justice of the peace, presides over the present case seemingly with consequentialist considerations in mind. He ties decisions to "fortune" rather than to any uncompromising principle. He prefers "pacience" to "rigour" (V.773–775), a distinction that resonates here. Should you be equally patient and accommodating?

In the end we find out that Dorigen is spared what seemed an inevitable shame: due to the knight Arveragus' apparent openhandedness, the squire Aurelius is unable to follow through with ravishing Dorigen. But for the time being the question posed by the Franklin must remain pertinent, since we do not know how things go. The dilemma is manifold at this contingent instant. Contingency itself can seem illusory, for the reader knows that the Franklin suspends events, *even as he superintends them*, postponing what he may know to be the case. Like the clerk-magician, he may be equipped with superior foreknowledge, making your judgement moot. The Franklin does come across as a somewhat reluctant adventurer, wishing to forestall one possible response to the tale so far. He does not want anyone thinking the knight is a "lewed man." It's a mildly apologetic gesture on his part. He guesses what you might think. His defensiveness may also indicate that he is ready to change course, opportunistically; he may alter events. The Franklin is a particularly meddlesome pilgrim after all: having once interrupted the Squire's tale, he now arrests his own. What then will he do now? Can anyone tell? He is also known as a convivial man, solicitous about the welfare of his guests, and so one implication is that he may resolve the situation to your satisfaction. Is the narrative fixed, rigged?

The Franklin aggravates matters by holding events in abeyance, putting you in an analogous situation to that of Dorigen, facing immanent disaster. The tale is one of emergent events that become *your* eventualities, where the truth is up for grabs. The situation is pressing because there is no access to the author (or Author-God). There is no divine or authorial assurance that things will turn out better, and even if they did (as in fact they *do*), the audience may find the ending an intolerable specimen of authorial inconstancy. The event is impossible to calculate, and no matter how it looks in retrospect (however stage-managed) the temporal unfolding of events remains eventful. It is in the nature of events to arrive as if from the future in this way: they only ever will have been — *future anterior*. In the meantime they suspend meaning, thwart expectation, surprise.[4]

§ MOST *FRE*?

What transpires directly following the Franklin's prevaricating remarks and request for readerly tolerance puts the situation in high relief, dramatizing what is at stake in assessing such hard realities. When Dorigen leaves her house

---

[4] Chaucer attains the suspense not by *foreshadowing* events to come so much as *sideshadowing*, creating a sort of middle realm containing a surplus of virtual possibilities. See Gary Saul Morson, *Narrative and Freedom: The Shadows of Time* (New Haven: Yale University Press, 1994), 6 et passim.

to meet Aurelius in the garden, she accidentally crosses paths with him in the town: "Of aventure happed hire to meete" (V.1501). A few lines later the meeting is described differently, "For wel he spyed whan she wolde go / Out of hir hous to any maner place" (V.1506–1507). Arveragus has in fact kept Dorigen under surveillance, and from his perspective, it was no chance meeting at all. Interestingly, the Franklin is evasive on the point, not wishing to commit one way or another, equivocating over the meaning of the intersecting lines of his own narration: "But thus they mette, of aventure or grace" (V.1508). His hedging cannot help but cast doubts on his role in the events. Is the Franklin, like Aurelius, not also taking pains to make luck go his way?

At the same time, the Franklin does not seem to know what he is saying. You may wonder if he knows where he is going, and whether the illusion is that he is in control. His equivocal response bears comparison with other notorious authorial asides, as in the *Nun's Priest's Tale* (VII.3252–3266), where the priest asserts and then retracts statements about women's counsel, in a dizzying and disingenuous series of *non sequiturs*, and also in the *Manciple's Tale* (IX.160–188), where the tale-teller issues a series of exempla about female fickleness that are subsequently construed, in an unexpectedly paranoid way, to apply to "men / That been untrewe, and nothyng by wommen" (IX.187–188). If there is anything to be said for the "roadside drama" approach to the *Canterbury Tales*, then it has to do with the theatrical way in which the pilgrims continually act and react, predict and pre-empt one another. The tale-telling game is an unfolding event, not a plot or program without the freedom to change direction. Here, perhaps, no doubt inadvertently again, something the Franklin said earlier seems material: "For in this world, certein, ther no wight is / That he ne dooth or seith somtyme amys" (V.79–80). In light of so much human error and ill fortune, what is anyone to do? Dorigen is not the only one who has misspoken — "in pley."

There seems an unavoidable "aventure" in the telling after all, some latitude to events. The tale's resolution is contingent on so many improbable, gratuitous gestures in fact. Here is how things go in the end. A husband is unexpectedly free (loose) with the body of his wife; a lover frees a woman of her (coerced) obligation; and finally a clerk releases a squire from a payment he could have never afforded to begin with. It is a tale ostensibly with so much *freedom* (outstripping *necessity*), where one gift elicits another in a kind of hastily assembled gift economy. The resolution turns on the multiple meanings of "fre," a word with a lot of semantic play.[5] The Franklin ends the tale with one final question, drawing you in to the debate: "Which was the mooste fre, as thynketh yow? / Now telleth me, er that ye ferther wende" (V.1620).

Of course freedom is always constrained by an identifiable sequence of cause and effect, which can be adduced here to explain the domino effect of the ending. A critique might run along these lines: real capital is not relinquished so much as counted up and cashed out to acquire symbolic goods. There is therefore no real gift without a demand for a return.[6] It is a decidedly masculinist orientation. Dorigen is an opportunity for men to show their truth, grace, and pity — a set of virtues that belong to what Auerbach would call a "class ethics" associated with the aristocracy.[7] The Franklin betrays his own class interest in the way the tale proceeds. He showed himself scrupulous about his patrimony in the interruption of the Squire (where the Franklin rebukes his son for wasting his

---

[5] Just a few of the relevant definitions of "fre" in the *Middle English Dictionary* include: "the status of a noble or a freeman"; "unrestricted in movement or action"; "free of the bonds of love or matrimony"; "unrestricted choice, the right or power to choose"; "noble in character; gracious, well-mannered"; "generous, open-handed"; "ready or willing."

[6] For an especially persuasive analysis, see Britton J. Harwood, "Chaucer and the Gift (If there is Any)," *Studies in Philology* 103.1 (2006): 26–46.

[7] Erich Auerbach, *Mimesis: The Representation of Reality in Western Literature*, trans. Willard R. Trask (Princeton: Princeton University Press, 1953), 138.

money and failing in decorum), and now seeks to distinguish himself as a free man, that is a franklin (from *franc*, free, in Old French), one who holds land in freehold and exercises aristocratic "franchise." To that end he sources a French or Italian story: a Breton lay or Boccaccian tale, demonstrating broad familiarity with the high-toned, cosmopolitan literature associated with the leisure class to which he aspires. Things can be explained away. The removal of the rocks was no natural disaster. A clerk arranged the events; the Franklin may have worked his magic too. You observe the patterns. The situation could be one big non-event. A cognitive reflex seems destined always to rationalize events: historicity becomes history; contingency, causality.

Events become relatively stable objects of retrospection and contemplation when treated to such critiques (i.e., construals of the truth), but that seems unwarranted in a tale about the instability and gratuity of events. Retrospection is delayed, belated, hard-won. We can hardly forget the affective dynamics and vicissitudes of the collective situation. We recall the fortunes to which husband, lover, and clerk are hostage. And who can neglect the suffering of Dorigen? Events are open-ended, catching characters off-guard, thwarting their plans. Respective outcomes are as much accidents as they are individual achievements, rising up from a phenomenal field of productivity that constitutes freedom as always partially determined. The audience is in no better position for the duration of the tale, and long afterward, having arrived at an ending that is unresolved ("fre"). The question with which the tale ends might actually be a most generous one: "Which was the mooste fre, as thynketh yow?" You assess the matter differently depending on where you find yourself in the event. That is close to the truth.

Black as the Crow

Travis Neel and Andrew Richmond

When Crow was white he decided the sun was too white.
He decided it glared much too whitely.
He decided to attack it and defeat it.

He got his strength up flush and in full glitter.
He clawed and fluffed his rage up.
He aimed his beak direct at the sun's centre.

He laughed himself to the centre of himself

And attacked.

At his battle cry trees grew suddenly old,
Shadows flattened.

But the sun brightened —
It brightened, and Crow returned charred black.

He opened his mouth but what came out was charred black.

"Up there," he managed,
"Where white is black and black is white, I won."

~Ted Hughes, "Crow's Fall"

Perched among the many birds in the *Parliament of Foules* sits "the crowe with vois of care" (364).[1] The crow receives no

---

[1] Quotations from the works of Geoffrey Chaucer are taken from *The*

space to speak in Geoffrey Chaucer's Valentine's Day poem —
a grim reminder perhaps of the circumstances under which he
received his sad voice and scorched appearance. In Chaucer's
hands it is a different, perhaps darker, story than the one told
by Ted Hughes. The crow does not launch himself into
blackness through a jealousy contest; rather he becomes but
one victim at the hands of a jealous and wrathful master. As
Chaucer's Manciple tells the story, the crow had once been a
white bird with a beautiful voice. Phoebus Apollo had taught
the crow how to speak like a human, and when this crow sang,
"Therwith in al this world no nyghtyngale/ Ne koude, by an
hondred thousand deel, / Syngen so wonder myrily and weel"
(IX.136–139). But the crow's status within Phoebus's
household does not last long in the *Manciple's Tale*. Having
witnessed Phoebus's wife with her beloved, the crow
immediately declares the wife's unfaithfulness to Phoebus —
and Pheobus' resulting identity as a cuckold — with the song,
"Cokkow! Cokkow! Cokkow!" (IX.243). Phoebus turns his ire
and sorrow towards his wife and his minstrelsy before
addressing the crow as a traitor. To quite the crow of his false
tale (IX.293), Phoebus strips him of his song, deplumes his
white feathers, and casts him out of his home.

But the *Manciple's Tale* does not conclude with the
etiology of the crow. Instead, the Manciple proclaims the crow
to be an example encouraging restraint in speech, especially
when telling a man about the sexual indiscretions of his wife
(IX.309–312). Echoing the advice of his mother, the Manciple
concludes by offering his audience the following injunction:
"Kepe wel thy tonge and thenk upon the crowe" (IX.362). The
critical reception of the *Manciple's Tale* has often followed the
Manciple's explication of his tale, noting that the analogy
between the Manciple and the bird might also extend to the

Riverside Chaucer, gen. ed. Larry D. Benson, 3rd edn. (Boston:
Houghton Mifflin, 1987), by line numbers (as well as by fragment
and book numbers, where applicable).

court poet.[2] For David Wallace, the *Manciple's Tale* demonstrates that Chaucer "never quite shakes off anxieties regarding the legitimacy or usefulness of his own social role."[3] Similarly, James Simpson writes,

> Chaucer marks the withdrawal of his own voice from the public realm with the story of Apollo's bird, who is punished for speaking the truth in terms rhetorically fit for base and scandalous actions. The narrative ends with the recommendation of silence, except in speaking about God; from the perspective of this tale, the following *Parson's Tale* is not so much salutary as safe.[4]

In her recent treatment of Chaucerian birds, Jill Mann echoes this line of critical reception, writing that, "A story of sexual betrayal thus becomes a story of linguistic betrayal."[5] For Mann and others, this linguistic betrayal is also a sign that the various communities represented by and within both the Manciple's prologue and his tale are highly fraught and

---

[2] Louise Fradenburg, "The Manciple's Servant Tongue: Politics and Poetry in *The Canterbury Tales*," *ELH* 52 (1985): 86 [85–118]. A. C. Spearing also suggests that the crow "is present as an impotent voyeur — precisely the role in which Chaucer so often places himself in his courtly poems about love" (*The Medieval Poet as Voyeur: Looking and Listening in Medieval Love-Narratives* [Cambridge, Eng.: Cambridge University Press, 1993], 137). Other approaches to the *Manciple's Tale* are exemplified in the six papers in the *Colloquium* on the *Manciple's Tale* in *Studies in the Age of Chaucer* 25 (2003): 287–337.

[3] David Wallace, *Chaucerian Polity: Absolutist Lineages and Associational Forms in England and Italy* (Stanford: Stanford University Press, 1997), 249.

[4] James Simpson, *The Oxford English Literary History, Volume 2, 1350-1547: Reform and Cultural Revolution* (Oxford: Oxford University Press, 2002), 253.

[5] Jill Mann, *From Aesop to Reynard: Beast Literature in Medieval Britain* (Oxford: Oxford University Press, 2009), 218

potentially dangerous.[6]

Yet, while the reception of the *Manciple's Tale* has done wonders to intimate the tensions and dangers of the poet-patron relationship, the tendency in these analyses has been to read the crow as an all-too-human servant.[7] The status of the crow as a bird, a pet, and one of the victims of Apollo's wrath enters the analytical frame only in as much as it is expressive of the anxieties of court servants. This essay aims to follow the latter part of the Manciple's ventriloquization of his mother's advice: to think on the crow. Rather than following the crow's metamorphosis from Chaucer's potential sources and analogues to the crow of Phoebus's house in the *Manciple's Tale*, we track the crow through the Chaucerian corpus.[8] The figure of the crow appears three times in Chaucer's works: silently perched alongside the raven in the *Parliament of Fowls*, as one of the victims in the *Manciple's Tale*, and as a metaphor for the very blackness of the blood streaming over Arcite's face near the conclusion to the *Knight's Tale*.[9] What marks these moments out to us is that whereas various late medieval texts offered a variety of possibilities for reading crows, Chaucer's

---

[6] Mann, *From Aesop to Reynard*, 218. For more on the social dangers represented in the *Manciple's Tale* see Fradenburg, "The Manciple's Servant Tongue"; Wallace, *Chaucerian Polity*; and Stephanie Trigg, "Friendship, Association, and Service in the *Manciple's Tale*," *Studies in the Age of Chaucer* 25 (2003): 325–330.

[7] Part of the inspiration for this pursuit was drawn from Jill Mann's confession that, "I cannot find that the role of the animal in the *Manciple's Tale* has been the central focus of attention in any analysis of the tale to date" (Mann, *From Aesop to Reynard*, 207 n36).

[8] For recent accounts of the possible sources and analogues to the *Manciple's Tale*, see Mann, 209–215, and Jamie C. Fumo, "Thinking upon the Crow: The *Manciple's Tale* and Ovidian Mythography," *The Chaucer Review* 38.4 (2004): 355–375.

[9] Arguably the crow could be said to make a fourth appearance in *Troilus and Criseyde* when Pandarus warns Criseyde about the effects of time by drawing her attention to what may be the first recorded use of "crowe's feet" (II.403).

crows are univocal in their dark significations. The crow marks what is abject in the games of love: the squawking of lesser fowls, the unfaithfulness of a lover, gossip, and treachery. In its darkest manifestations, the crow becomes a marker for silence, sterility, and death. To think on the crow is not to dwell in one of the darkest tales of Chaucer's *Canterbury Tales*; it is to dwell with the darkness generated by that tale. The Chaucerian crow testifies that participation in the *desportes* of love necessitates the production of abject bodies and spaces: "And for this caas been alle crowes blake" (IX.307).

While Chaucer's crow may register only a dark signification, the crow as described in a variety of other high and late medieval works emerges as an ambiguous character.[10] Naturalistic accounts detailed an animal exemplifying a strong familial instinct, while theological treatises presented a bird burdened with dark associations to the Devil and prophecy. Throughout this spectrum of texts, a common refrain concentrates on attributing a strong sense of worldliness to the crow. For instance, Hugh of Fouilley opens his *Aviarum* (twelfth century) by contrasting the Psalmic beauty of the dove with the black raven, whose cry of *cras, cras* [tomorrow, tomorrow] reveals its eternal desire for one more day of life on earth.[11] The crow was also said to use this same cry, and thus to subscribe to the accompanying conceit.[12] Indeed, this

---

[10] Since the Middle English word "croue" or "crowe" was often used to refer to both crows and ravens, our discussion of the crow has been somewhat supplemented (particularly in theological contexts) with discussions of the raven; see *MED*, "croue (n.)," meaning 1(a).

[11] W.B. Clark, ed. and trans., *The Medieval Book of Birds: Hugh of Fouilloy's* Aviarum (Binghamton: Medieval and Renaissance Texts and Studies, 1992) 117.

[12] For instance, Isidore of Seville (seventh century) remarks that "many bird names are evidently constructed from the sound of their calls, such as . . . the crow (*corvus*)": S.A. Barney et al., eds. and trans., *The* Etymologies *of Isidore of Seville* (Cambridge, Eng.: Cambridge University Press, 2006), 264.

tradition may have influenced the belief that crows lived to achieve great age. Early modern texts posit that crows would take one mate for life, exemplifying marital fidelity and concord.[13] The crow was also thought to be a devoted family bird, caring for its offspring long after they had left the nest. Albertus Magnus (twelfth century) notes that such an attitude towards their youth was motivated by a sense of piety.[14] In a defensive capacity, crows were well known for antagonizing birds of prey, particularly eagles and owls, gathering into groups to overcome their stronger foes.[15] However, crow parents were believed to refrain from caring for newborn chicks until their complexion was appropriately darkened; before they were black, the parents could not recognize them as fellow crows. According to Caxton's *Mirror of the World,* this concentration on color as the primary marker of crow-identity derives from the fact that the crow believed itself to be the fairest of all birds in appearance and voice.[16] Finally, while white crows were known, this was often taken to be a sign of disease or weakness, not as a sign of Divine favor.[17]

In theological contexts, crows and ravens often served to represent two sides of the same coin. Hugh of Fouilley's account details how ravens mimic the assault of the Devil by first going for the eyes of corpses, entering thereby into the

---

[13] E. Topsell, *The Fowles of Heauen or History of Birdes,* eds. T.P. Harrison and F.D. Hoeniger (Austin: University of Texas Press, 1972), 224–225 (citing primarily Classical sources).

[14] K.F. Kitchell, Jr., and I.M. Resnick, trans., *Albertus Magnus On Animals: A Medieval Summa Zoologica,* Vols. 1 & 2 (Baltimore: Johns Hopkins University Press, 1999), 1567.

[15] Kitchell and Resnick, *Albertus Magnus on Animals,* 672, 1567.

[16] O.H. Prior, *Caxton's Mirror of the World,* Early English Texts Society, e.s. 110 (London, UK: Kegan Paul, Trench, Trubner & Co., Ltd., 1913), 103. Caxton translated a French text, *Image du Monde*, which had been in circulation since the thirteenth century; see Prior, *Caxtoun's Mirrour,* v-vi.

[17] Kitchell and Resnick, *Albertus Magnus on Animals*, 1352.

brain.[18] Genesis 8:7 provided further support for the theory of the raven and crow as worldly birds, stating that the bird did not return to Noah's Ark when sent to search for land. As such, ravens and crows were seen to represent worldly sinners, lacking the ability for introspection. Their black plumage was thus taken as symbolic of despair, of sinners that had lost all hope for God's grace.[19] Yet their darkness could also be seen as indicative of humility, the black raven representing a good preacher, who wears the memory of his sins in his black cloth. In this light, then, the parental activities of crows and ravens could be interpreted positively: the parents waited for their children to turn black before caring for them, just as good prelates waited for their students to demonstrate humility before accepting them.[20] Finally, crows were well known as birds used by pagan augury, and their cry was commonly held to be indicative of coming rain.[21]

Lodged between reflecting the life of a real-world animal and symbolizing carnal desire, the late medieval crow resisted becoming a simple marker of danger or dark fate. Rather, the attributes of fidelity, concord, and familial responsibility especially defined the crow as a heuristic of properly monogamous, reproductive morality. In love, then, the crow's worldliness was balanced by a devotion to duty and propagation that favored the protection of mate and kin above all other obligations — a surprising character twist on the common villain of battlefield carrion-feeders. Worldly and considerate, humble and vain, the crow's singular color belied a wide palette of associations from which a late medieval author could draw.

---

[18] Clark, *The Medieval Book of Birds,* 175. See also Kitchell and Resnick, *Albertus Magnus on Animals,* 600, for Albertus Magnus's categorization of crows as omnivorous.

[19] Clark, *The Medieval Book of Birds,* 177.

[20] Clark, *The Medieval Book of Birds,* 177–179.

[21] Kitchell and Resnick, *Albertus Magnus on Animals,* 1567; Barney et al., *The Etymologies of Isidore of Seville,* 267.

In Chaucer's hands, however, the polysemic possibilities of
the crow become narrower and darker. Perched alongside the
raven in the *Parliament of Foules*, Chaucer has put the crow in
his place. While the crow and the raven may be among the
noise of fowls that cry for an end to the argument (491–497),
their singular voices are never heard. When Nature silences
the "murmur of the lewednesse behynde" (520), there is no
sense that the crow has spoken out of turn with his "vois of
care." In this game of love, the crow has but one duty: to
watch silently. This impotent voyeurism is often discussed in
treatments of the crow in the *Manciple's Tale*, where the
crow's silence as he watches the betrayal of Apollo's mistress is
contrasted with his bursting forth in speech upon Apollo's
return.[22] In these contexts, Apollo's judgment that the crow is
a traitor who has spoken a fals tale suggests that the crow
might be — as the Manciple glosses — an exemplar for proper
and tactful speech.

But Apollo's crow, like the crow of the *Parliament*, is in a
no-win situation. Silence would seem to make him complicit
in the wife's infidelity, and speech only seems to lead to
trouble. The crow's crime seems not to be what he speaks or
how he speaks, but rather that he speaks at all. The crow's
initial cry to Apollo ("Cokkow") reveals itself to be multiply
transgressive. The onomatopoetic utterance invokes both the
call of Apollo's beloved pet and the vulgar speech of a
household servant. From any other crow, this utterance might
not signal any cause for alarm, but this bird had been taught
to counterfeit human speech. What comes out of his mouth,
then, is unrecognizable — except that it is damning. More
importantly, though, the crow confronts Apollo and the
audience of the *Manciple's Tale* with the possibility that the

---

[22] Spearing, *The Medieval Poet as Voyeur,* 137. John McCall describes
the crow as "stupid, insensitive, blabbering, short-sighted, and
voyeuristic" in *Chaucer Among the Gods: The Poetics of Classical
Myth* (University Park: Pennsylvania State University Press, 1979),
148.

tale is not a romance, but a fabliau — that Apollo is not a
romantic hero, but a cuckolded husband.[23]

In order to re-establish the ordered household and the
identity of the romantic hero that the Manciple presents his
audiences with at the start of the tale, Apollo must purge both
his person and his home of every stain that would contradict
his claims to "gentillesse, honour and parfit worthinesse"
(IX.124–125). While the Manciple and a very large and
heavily substantiated cross-section of the secondary literature
on his tale suggests that the crow's transgression is intimately
tied to language and the proper uses of speech, we would
suggest that the crow's role in the tale cannot simply be
reduced to a stand-in for a household servant, for the
narrators, or for Chaucer himself. Rather, the crow of the
Manciple's Tale manifests the abject — the unstable boundary
where subject and object confront one another and meaning
risks collapse. While Apollo takes out his jealous rage on his
wife, instruments, and crow respectively, the focus of both his
rage and the Manciple's narration fall squarely upon the
figure of the crow and his becoming-black. Despite the avowal
that "ther is namoore to sayn" after Apollo murders his wife,
the *Manciple's Tale* continues to describe how Apollo
displaces his sorrow, guilt, and rage onto the crow: "Traitor,'
quod he, 'with tonge of scorpioun,/ Thou hast me broght to
my confisioun;" (IX.266, 271–272). The crow, who — like
the wife — had begun the tale as one of the prized love-objects
of the romantic hero, remains structurally linked to Apollo's
wife as the hero and the tale struggle to deny and to reject all
of the narrative's fabliaux elements. The now-dead wife is
linked to the still living crow in a contrast between the
traitor's false tongue and the dead lover's innocence: "O deere
wyf! O gemme of lusti-heed! / That were to me so sad and eek

---

[23] Ann Astell, "Nietzsche, Chaucer, and the Sacrifice of Art," *The
Chaucer Review* 39.3 (2005): 323–340. Many have noted that the
Manciple's Tale struggles to pose as a chivalric romance but gives
way even in the beginning to the tones of fabliau.

so trewe, / Now listow deed, with face pale of hewe, / Ful giltelees, that dorste I swere, ywys!" (IX.274–277). Apollo's final attention to the wife is significant here in two respects. First, the concluding scenes of the *Manciple's Tale* omit elements of its Ovidian source: the wife's name, her speech, the revelation of her pregnancy, and the presence of her lifeless body as Apollo rescues their son from her womb.[24] Second, Apollo's lament for his wife reinforces the structural link between her and the crow. The pale hue of his wife's corpse is the final glimpse (IX.275) offered of the wife as Apollo's vengeance on the crow becomes the central feature of the tale.[25]

In the short space of thirty-eight lines (IX.270–308), the crow becomes a loaded signifier: traitor, false thief, black, silent, and the structural parallel to an absent corpse bereft of its offspring. Having accused the crow of treachery (IX.270) and implicated him in the act of murder (IX.271–272), Apollo proceeds to curse the crow:

"O false theef!" seyde he,
"I wol thee quite anon thy false tale.
Thou songe whilom lyk a nyghtyngale;
Now shaltow, false theef, thy song forgon,
And eek thy white fetheres everichon,
Ne nevere in al thy lif ne shaltou speke.
Thou shal men on a traytour been awreke;
Thou and thyn ofspryng evere shul be blake
Ne nevere sweete noyse shul ye make,

---

[24] For discussions of these omissions see Jamie C. Fumo, "Thinking upon the Crow," and the papers in the Colloquium on the *Manciple's Tale* in *Studies in the Age of Chaucer* 25 (2003), particularly John Hines, "For sorwe of which he brak his minstralcye": The Demise of the 'Sweete Noyse' of Verse in the *Canterbury Tales*," 302 [299–308].
[25] See Astell, "Nietzsche, Chaucer, and the Sacrifice of Art," 329 and 332, for a description of the crow as a scapegoat.

But evere crie agayn tempest and rayn,
In tokenynge that thurgh thee my wyf is slayn."
(IX.290–302)

Here, Apollo takes advantage of the non-human crow's human attribute (rational speech) to expunge the sin of his own murderous action. Yet the crow is simultaneously recognizable through his physical attributes (most notably, white feathers) as a non-human animal, an object compelled to suffer the course of Apollo's rehabilitation of romantic identity. Apollo denies the animality inhering in both his wife (the metaphor of the guilded cage, IX.162) and himself, and ascribes these bad traits to the "true" animal, the crow. Black was the deed, and black the crow shall be, "in tokenynge that thurgh thee my wyf is slayn." Apollo castigates the crow "And pulled his white fetheres everychon, / And made hym blak, and refte hym al his song, / And eek his speche, and out at dore hym slong / Unto the devel" (IX.303–305). Apollo further clarifies this goal of displacing all the animal traits onto the crow by transforming his voice into speech that shall be "nevere sweet noyse . . . / but evere crie agayn tempest and rayn" — the forces of the nonhuman, natural world. In this way, Apollo seeks to force the marginal crow — figure of the abject — into the separate other, forcing him "out at dore" (IX.306), imbued now with Apollo's violence, the wife's unfaithfulness, and the univocal cockow appropriate to a bird "with vois of care." Signaling a shift from failed romance and fabliaux to beast fable, the metamorphosis of the crow offers the *Manciple's Tale* the possibility of being read etiologically. This is, in fact, the direction that the Manciple takes as he turns to the company of pilgrims with the gloss: "And for this caas been alle crowes blake" (IX.307).

   In this way, the crow of the *Manciple's Tale* manifests the abject — the unstable boundary where subject and object confront one another, and meaning risks collapse. In a language particularly reminiscent of Apollo's crow, Julia Kristeva describes the abject as

> what disturbs identity, system, order. What does not respect borders, positions, rules. The in-between, the ambiguous, the composite. The traitor, the liar, the criminal with a good conscience, the shameless rapist, the killer who claims he is a savior.[26]

The abjection of the other (Apollo's metamorphosis of the crow and the Manciple's erasure of the corpse from his tale) serves to defend the subject from a collapse of the symbolic. In Apollo's eyes, the crow must take on all of the traits that would deny the possibility of becoming a romantic hero. The crow must not only become dark and speechless, but he must also be clearly marked as an animal and stand in for the corpse that in hindsight Apollo wishes he had not produced. In this light, it is not surprising that the crow's feathers are first mentioned as they are being pulled (IX.304) and that the crow is consigned to the devil as though he were already dead (IX.307). In his final image of the crow, then, the Manciple offers a figure "on the edge of nonexistence."[27]

We encounter the third figure of the crow in Chaucer's corpus at yet another instance of such a figure — the bloody face of the dying Arcita in Part Four of the *Knight's Tale*. Before Arcita dies at the end of the *Knight's Tale*, Chaucer offers a lingering depiction of Arcita's wounds that begins with an invocation of the crow:

> His brest tobrosten with his sadel-bowe.
> As blak he lay as any cole or crowe,
> So was the blood yronnen in his face.

---

[26] Julia Kristeva, *Powers of Horror: An Essay on Abjection*, trans. Leon S. Roudiez (New York: Columbia University Press, 1982), 4.

[27] Kristeva, *Powers of Horror: An Essay on Abjection*, 2. Chaucer's crow may not be abjected in the truest sense of Kristeva's usage since she writes, "there is nothing either objective or objectal to the abject" (9). It might be suggested that the crow could be read as a "deject," or as the product of a sublimation aiming at controlling a more primal repression (10–13).

Anon he was yborn out of the place,
With herte soor, to Theseus paleys. (I.2691–2695)

The confluence of the crumbling of literary artifice, the intrusion of the natural into the courtly, and the figure of the crow coalesce in the moment of the hero's body-becoming-corpse. Arcita's impending death nearly robs the *Knight's Tale* of its romantic ending by posing the possibility of courtly tragedy — a dramatic cleavage that the Knight spends the rest of his tale seeking to resolve. Only through the machinations of Theseus is the romance rescued from its tragic potentials, as Emelye is promised to Palamoun and the tale can finally conclude as romance. On the edge of generic collapse, then, the crow emerges fully abjected as a figure of the very blackness of the blood that marks Arcita as being between two deaths.[28] While Apollo's crow may only parallel the wife's corpse, the Knight's crow foretells of a corpse to come. Rather than black being a descriptor of the crow, the figure of the crow becomes an explication for how darkly Arcita's blood runs. The Knight's comparison transforms the crow into a description of the color and a sure sign that there will be no remedy for Arcita's latest heartbreak. The crow's colorful possibilities are confined in Chaucer's poetry to blackness, foreboding blood, the becoming-corpse.

Thinking upon Chaucer's crow draws us to the boundaries: included in the parliament but consigned to silence, taught to speak in order to be muted, conferred to the devil while still alive, caught between serving in a romance or suffering in a fabliau, and running down a not-yet-dead face. Like the absent body of Apollo's wife, the indecipherable but offensively clear utterance of "Cokkow," the voyeuristic presence of lesser fowls, or the blood streaming from a mortal wound, Chaucer's crow is a dark and ominous figure. The

---

[28] For an attentive reading of the "cole or crowe" simile, see L.O. Aranye Fradenburg, *Sacrifice Your Love: Psychoanalysis, Historicism, Chaucer* (Minneapolis: University of Minnesota Press, 2002), 167.

blackened crow remains a token of the animal within, the traitor in our midst, the body-becoming-corpse, and the white bird whose truthfulness was condemned to blackness. It is this constant abjection of the crow that the Manciple — following his mother — calls us never to forget as we continue to "thenk on the crowe" (IX.319, 362). But what makes the crow's presence perhaps more haunting is the remembrance of a different time — a time when black was white, "Cokkow" was sung in the voice unmatched by nightingales, lovers were true, and the blood shed by a chivalrous knight was not life-threatening. Possibly, then, Chaucer's crow hearkens us to a primordial time — where the crow wins. Where white is black and black is white, where thinking on the crow facilitates an enjoyment that is not abject, Chaucer's crow might be beautifully unrecognizable.

Unravelling Constance

Hannah Priest

She seyde she was so mazed in the see
That she forgat hir mynde, by hir trouthe.
~Chaucer, *The Man of Law's Tale*

She came from the sea, mazed, amazed — *masen* —confused,
bewildered, senseless. Deceived, deranged, crazed. They
stopped and asked her who she was. When they stopped and
asked her who she was, she said she did not know. She said
she was so mazed in the sea, that she forgot her mind. Her
mind — *mynde* — seat of memory, faculty of memory,
individual remembrance. Reason, understanding. Will, desire,
purpose. She forgot her mind, when she lost herself.
Constance forgets Constance. Constance is lost. Distress
teaches us to be inventive, says the nightingale, but blank
Constance does not invent.[1]

Once, she was Constance. Syrian chapmen found her in
Rome, among the other things, specially. The chapmen took
their cloths of gold, their satins rich of hew, their chaffare so

---

[1] I am grateful to Christina Petty and Janilee Plummer, postgraduate
students on the Lexis of Cloth and Clothing Project at the University
of Manchester, for their advice on matters relating to medieval
embroidery and cloth production.

thrifty and new, and returned with tales of Constance. Their chaffare — anything of virtue, something desirable. An exchange, a bargain, a deal. So thrifty — well-made, seemly, suitable. Golden, rich of hew, so thrifty and so new, they returned with tales of Constance. The chapmen went to market. Take the cloth and sell the cloth, take the goods and sell the goods. The smooth trade in luxury prevails over gods and geography. Facilitate allegiance in the market. Chapmen exchange satin for Dame Constance.

But now she comes from the sea, so mazed that she forgot her mind. Constance forgotten.

Take the cloth and pull the threads, unravelling the stitches. The picture isn't woven, it can be undone. Stitches unpicked from the linen cloth, one thread at a time. Wind the silks around your hand, little by little erase. Fine scissors cut again and again, and the silks are all removed. The picture isn't woven, and it can be undone. But look — small holes and blemishes, silk smudges and colours remain. Wash the cloth well. Soak it in water. All traces of the picture are gone. The cloth can be reused.

Constance meets another, a woman wrapped in cloth. She says I have forgot my mind. The other holds a fine needle and a piece of fine spun gold. Constance says I am a wretch — *wrecca* — outcast, exiled. The other says I am Egaré — *esgarée* — outcast, exiled. And the cloth on her shone so bright. They asked me for my name, she says, and I changed it there anon. She takes the needle and couches gold over layers of silk, embellishing, embroidering. A cloth, a story, a name. Constance has no needle. Her cloth is bare, and there is nothing there to couch. Blank linen, no trace of what came before.

Egaré shows her another woman. From somewhere further east. This woman makes a love-token to give to a Sultan's son. She takes the cloth and covers it in gold and azure, rich stones on every side. She adds pictures to the corners. Lovers, separated, suffering. Her web charts grief beyond her own. In the fourth, she weaves herself, her lover, to testify their tale. To bear witness, manifest, and attest the truth. Love token bestowed turns to spoil of war, and ends in the hands of an emperor. Egaré wraps herself in the woven words of the Eastern weaver, and coats herself in the testament. When the storms rage at sea, she will use unforgotten stories to cover her own face.

And now another comes. She says her name is Couste. I am a woman woefully bestad, says Constance, I have forgot my mind. I am a woman woefully bestad, says Couste. They asked me for my name, she says, but I would not confess. I keep it woven into me, a cloth, a story, a name. Couste can be recognized, through the traces of my tale. In the word I choose to mean myself, my self-fashioned me, not all stitches can be unpicked. But Constance has no tapestry. The frame is bare, and there is nothing here to weave. Blank linen, no trace of what was there before.

Take the cloth and pull the threads, unravelling the stitches. The picture isn't woven, it can be undone. Stitches unpicked from the linen cloth, one thread at a time. Wind the silks around your hand, little by little erase. Fine scissors cut again and again, and the silks are all removed. The picture isn't woven, and it can be undone. But look – small holes and blemishes, silk smudges and colours remain. Wash the cloth well. Soak it in water. All traces of the picture are gone. The cloth can be reused.

A nightingale weaves a tapestry. In her youth she had learned to work and to embroider. To weave in her frame a radevore, as she knows women did of yore. She weaves, I am a woeful lady. Constance says, I am a woeful lady. I have forgot my mind. The nightingale stitches, with a pen I cannot write, but I can weave letters to and fro. It takes a year to fill my wooden frame, but then I weave it well. My cloth, my story, my name, and how I was served for my sister's love. To bear witness, manifest, and to attest the truth.

Constance sees the nightingale's cloth. Woollen threads complete the wooden frame. No threads remain of Constance now. No letters woven on a frame. How is she served for her father's love? How is she served for her husband's love? I do not sew, says Constance, I do not weave. Who are you? weaves the nightingale. I do not remember. I cannot testify.

A Greek bird sews the scene the same, though her dumb lips cannot reveal. But grief and pain might breed ingenuity, and distress teaches us to be inventive. Constance suffers grief and pain, and her dumb lips do not reveal. But no ingenuity remains with her, inventiveness unthreaded and washed away. She stitches no scene, she weaves no letters. She has no needle, she has no name.

Take the cloth and pull the threads, unravelling the stitches. The picture isn't woven, it can be undone. Stitches unpicked from the linen cloth, one thread at a time. Wind the silks around your hand, little by little erase. Fine scissors cut again and again, and the silks are all removed. The picture isn't woven, and it can be undone. But look — small holes and blemishes, silk smudges and colours remain. Wash the cloth

well. Soak it in water. All traces of the picture are gone. The
cloth can be reused.

The chapmen took their cloths of gold, their satins rich of
hew, their chaffare so thrifty and new, and returned with tales
of Constance. Golden, rich of hew, so thrifty and so new. She
has no needle to embroider her cloth, and she has no shears to
cut it. Her threads were pulled by other hands, by many pairs
of other hands.

A Sultaness, a cursed crone, first does the cursed deed.
Constance's act of embroidery, sewing Christian yarns on
Syrian cloth, is stopped before the needle pricks. The old
woman measures the threads of her son's life, and snaps her
shears early. The crone's Syrian tapestry remains unchanged
and Constance unravelling is given to the sea.

Donegild, next, full of tyranny. Her daughter-in-law's cloth is
ready for images to be sewn, and the patterns are now set. But
the old queen waits with her own silk, to counterfeit most
subtly. Her picture she wrought most sinfully, as she
embroiders Constance's monstrosity. She unpicks the words
that her son might say, and invents a new story. The old
queen's skill outstrips the younger's and Constance
unravelling is given to the sea.

Stitchcraft is taught woman to girl. Without a mother, a nurse
will do (maybe a lady that men call Abro). Constance says
goodbye to her mother, and never learns to sew. It is no
marvel, then, that crones and queens can wield their needles
with far more subtlety. Constance lacks their skill. She has no
needle, she has no name.

Take the cloth and pull the threads, unravelling the stitches. The picture isn't woven, it can be undone. Stitches unpicked from the linen cloth, one thread at a time. Wind the silks around your hand, little by little erase. Fine scissors cut again and again, and the silks are all removed. The picture isn't woven, and it can be undone. But look — small holes and blemishes, silk smudges and colours remain. Wash the cloth well. Soak it in water. All traces of the picture are gone. The cloth can be reused.

Two women weave tapestries and grieve. One, alone and lonely, sews a funeral robe. She weaves the great web all day. But when night comes she sets torches beside her, and unravels her own stitches. The other, alone and lonely, weaves by night and day a magic web with colours gay. Did you write your name upon the boat? she says. Did you write it on the prow? Go to your house, and busy yourself. Go to your distaff and loom. I have no house, Constance says. I am a wretch — *wrecca* — outcast and exiled. I have no distaff and I have no loom. I have no warp and I have no weft. I have no web to weave.

Look to the spider, Constance. From her belly, she yet spins her thread, and as a spider is busy with her web of old. Grief and pain might breed ingenuity, and distress teaches her to be inventive. The spider's web charts grief beyond her own. Europa, Asterie, Antiope. Alcmene, Danae, Aegina. Proserpine, Canace, Iphimedeia. Bisaltis, Demeter, Melantho. Medusa, Isse, Erigone. Egaré and Couste, the daughter of the Emir. The nightingale, Ithaca's queen, the lady in the tower. Other women have been mazed before. Deceived, deranged, crazed. Other women have been mazed before. But they kept hold of the threads to find the way out.

Constance. Constance has no place inside a web. She cannot sew her self. She has no web, she has no loom. She has no silk, she has no gold. She has no needles, she has no frame. She is the cloth that the chapmen bought. She is the cloth for crones and queens to couch upon. The cloth for kings and Sultans to couch gold upon. She is the blank linen back without the wool, the unpicked square without the yarn.

She has no memory, she has no mind. She has no needle, she has no name. She has no warp, she has no weft. No testament, no tapestry.

Take the cloth and pull the threads, unravelling the stitches. The picture isn't woven, it can be undone. Stitches unpicked from the linen cloth, one thread at a time. Wind the silks around your hand, and little by little erase. Fine scissors cut again and again, and the silks are all removed. The picture isn't woven, and it can be undone. But look — small holes and blemishes, silk smudges and colours remain. Wash the cloth well. Soak it in water. All traces of the picture are gone. The cloth can be reused.

She came from the sea, mazed, amazed. An exchange, a bargain, a deal. They stopped and asked her who she was. When they stopped and asked her who she was, she said she did not know. Golden, rich of hew, so thrifty and so new. She said she was so mazed in the sea, that she forgot her mind. Reason, understanding, will, desire, purpose. Go to your distaff and loom. Constance forgot Constance. Constance is lost.

⊛ L'O de V: A Palimpsest

Lisa Schamess

> Pornography, like fairy tale, tells us who we are.
> ~Andrea Dworkin

> There is also something called a poire prisonnière. Unlike other eaux-de-vie, poire prisonnière captures the fruit itself. Early in the growing season, when the pears are just forming on the trees, glass bottles are tied over some of the most promising buds. The pear grows inside the bottle, and when it is ripe, it is cut from the tree-still in the bottle. Both bottle and pear are washed and pear brandy is added. The whole pear is in the bottle you buy, its beauty and flavor completely intact.
> ~ "Eaux de Vie (Eau de Vie)," *Moveable Feasts*[1]

The photo of Poire Prisonnière is from Westford Distilleries (http://www. westfordhill.com), reprinted here with their permission.

[1] "Eaux de Vie (Eau de Vie)," *Moveable Feasts* [cookbook weblog], March 27, 2010: http://moveablefeastscookbook.blogspot.com/2010/ 03/eaux-de-vie-

§ Heere folweth the Phisiciens Tale.

~~For centuries she didn't speak at all, the girl Virginia.~~ *The silent girl who finally speaks tells the story. Submission, omission, commission, submersion, subversion, inversion, corruption, coercion. Defilement, denial, the child, the trial, fil, fille, vile, ville, filial bonds, bondage, twisted positions and impositions, text and subtext and context and cuntext. Penetration, vellum, hide, marks, pens, wounds, piercings, cuttings, severings, maidenheads, giving head, what's inside our heads that is left unsaid, what cannot be said being said, the sinkhole in a prison bed, the outburst of consent and the pressure of speech,* the hand holding the pencil raced over the paper without the least concern for the hour or the light. The girl was writing the way you speak in the dark to the person you love when you've held back the words of love too long and they flow at last[2], *hysteria catatonia silence asceticism abasement how a woman throws herself is thrown hurls herself is hurled cuts herself is cut how there is an O in the center of the monastery and in the rear of the prison the text is inscribed, marked, stripped, cut, scraped, erased, reinscribed, corrected, raped, rapt, wrapped[3] and how this story is old, begins with a snake's mouth and ends in a bit of tale served up by a woman, an O, once a V, an A(nne), an A(ury), a Pauline nun from the*

---

eau-de-vie.html.

[2] Pauline Réage, née Anne Desclos, *alias* Dominique Aury, *Return to the Chateau, preceded by, A Girl in Love* (New York: Grove Press, 1973), 7.

[3] Parallels between the body and text have been drawn by many scholars and poets, including Chaucer. Carolyn Dinshaw illuminates the relation of text and subjugated female body in *Chaucer's Sexual Poetics* (Madison: University of Wisconsin, 1989), citing Chaucer's use of the then-ambiguous word "rape" in his "Chaucer's Wordes unto Adam, His Owne Scriveyn": The final line, "And al is thorough thy negligence and rape," could mean merely haste and carelessness or, as was current by Chaucer's time, could at least connote the modern meaning of sexual violation. Dinshaw argues that Chaucer deployed the ambiguity with deliberate intent to invest the word and the subject of writing and text-making with a gendered, sexual meaning (3–10).

bawdy papers, a Reagent. The Autre. The ~~Autre~~[4] *Translation transgression transubstantiation,* trasumanar[5]*, tongues, longing, language, sources, apocrypha apostasy outtakes originals pens and penetration, comments, commas, parents, parentheses, prisons, patrimony, patronage, the mouth, the eye, the os, the ass, the orifice, the vacuole, the caesura, the fissure, the seizure, the rapture,* ravissement, *stripping away, strips of skin, laceration, O in the middle,* jouissance,[6] *O behind, the iron O on the finger, the steel O in the labia, the monsters inside us: The Three-Legged Man, The Headless Woman . . . we forget to remember and remember to forget a story of giving credit and revoking credit of not knowing half the time to whom to give credit.*[7]

---

[4] "In Lacanian terms, the other — the 'barred' O — is what lies behind the fantasy of the full, watchful Other. This 'barred' O can never be fully accounted for . . . [and] is one way of designating the 'symbolic order,' the open-ended and unpredictable network of signifiers that constructs human subjectivity," writes L.O. Aranye Fradenburg, *Sacrifice Your Love: Psychoanalysis, Historicism, and Chaucer* (Minneapolis: University of Minnesota Press, 2002), 5–6.

[5] "Trasumanare" is generally agreed to have been coined by Dante in Canto I, line 70 of *The Paradiso*, and has been translated to mean, "to transcend the human." The word's inexpressible meaning is articulated at its very birth in the phrase "Trasumanar significar per verba / Non si poria" ["The passing beyond humanity cannot be described in words," I.70–71], as cited by Mariann Sanders Regan in *Love Words: The Self and the Text in Medieval and Renaissance Poetry* (Ithaca: Cornell University Press, 1982), 174.

[6] An untranslatable word from the French for extreme (and usually sexual) bliss characterized by "a pleasure that is excessive, leading to a sense of being overwhelmed or disgusted, yet simultaneously providing a source of fascination": Bruce Fink, *The Lacanian Subject: Between Language and Jouissance* (Princeton: Princeton University Press, 1995), xii. Lacan took up the term circa 1959 to describe desire of the most fundamental sort, and to this day a good way to start a bloodbath among Lacanians is to release a little *jouissance* into the water. For one rather heady and gutsy discussion, see Adrian Johnston, "The Forced Choice of Enjoyment: Jouissance Between Expectation and Actualization," *Lacan.com* [n.d.], http://www.lacan.com/forced.htm.

[7] This opening monologue owes its trajectory to Lucky's speech in Beckett's *Waiting for Godot*.

Take. Eat.[8]

She listened from another room or sat sewing in the same room, as her father praised her to the suitors, calling their attention to her modesty, her chastity, her health, her clean habits and orderly mind. *As wel in goost as body chast was she.* The father boasted that she was fully obedient and flexible to his discipline, and *"Who is she," they were saying, "who does she belong to?" "You, if you like," he replied,*[9] that a good husband would have no difficulty at all containing her youth and impulsiveness. In fact, these qualities so little plagued her, that she might instruct another in sobriety.

(This is a corrupt text.)

Another version of this essay's beginning is simpler and more direct.[10]

The daughter's consent.[11]

From the first known telling of the crime of Appius and the

---

[8] Within an apocryphal version of Genesis, a curious tale links nourishment with penitence and sacrificial killing of a woman by a man, at the woman's request. To which the man — The Man, Adam — does not consent, saying, "How indeed, can I do you any evil, for you are my body." The first attempt at communion, exiled from the Bible itself in the slushpile of apocrypha (see Gary A. Anderson and Michael E. Stone, *The Life of Adam and Eve: The Biblical Story in Judaism and Christianity*: http://www2.iath.virginia.edu/anderson/vita/english/vita.arm.html#per2). Also not forgetting the role of eating in sacramental moments of the Church and in the moments of treachery against virgins in stories such as *Snow White*, as well as the details of the Frog Prince in which the Princess's bowl and cup are as important to the Frog as her bed.

[9] Pauline Réage, *Story of O* (New York: Ballantine Books, 1973), 197.

[10] Paraphrase from Réage, *Story of O*, 5.

[11] Lianna Farber states, "In a remarkable moment of the *Physician's Tale* Virginia consents to her own death, asking her father Virginius to kill her: "Yif me my deeth, er that I have a shame," she implores him (VI.249). This moment, like all those when Virginia speaks, appears neither in Chaucer's stated source, Livy's history, which Chaucer may or may not have known, nor in his unstated source, Jean de Meun's *Roman de la Rose*, which Chaucer most certainly did know" ("The Creation of Consent in the Physician's Tale," *The Chaucer Review* 39.2 [2004]: 151–164).

honor-killing of the girl Virginia,[12] certain traits survive into subsequent retellings. Chaucer's "The Physician's Tale" is part of a trio of medieval recountings that include Reason's assertions to the Lover in *Le Roman de la Rose* and John Gower's roughly concurrent and possibly competitive retelling in *Confessio amantis*. All three preserve Livy's essential triangle of lustful judge (Appius), loyal soldier who defies the law (Virginius), and hapless virgin whose physical life is taken by her father to preserve her chastity (Virginia).

But an entire person is missing from *Le Roman de la Rose* and from Chaucer's story: Lucius Icilius, to whom Virginia was lawfully betrothed in Livy's telling. Chaucer's version also tweaks a passing detail in Livy's original: she was apprehended by the judge's man as she went to school in Livy, whereas Chaucer inserts a temple. Both changes set the girl on an ascent from person to quality, from Virginia to V.

The removal of Icilius from the narrative, first in *Le Roman* and later in Chaucer's tale, may have been a simple choice for editorial expediency, but it acts as a ritual purification.[13] The Xing out of a future husband transubstantiates the girl from marriageable young woman to sacred object, Christlike as her father's only child. Then the sacrifice of her to prevent her defilement by Appius becomes allegorical, her day in kangaroo court as absurd as Jesus's trial before Pilate. Her pleading, her swooning, and her eventual acceptance of her father's will suggest Christ's passion on the cross, a parallel that is both supported and profaned by the follow-up pairing with the Pardoner, with his mocked-up relics, his rags and bones, and his trio of rogues who cancel themselves in their quest to cancel Death.

Most important, Virginia never speaks in any version until Chaucer adds her consent to her own death, albeit after protestations and a few fainting spells: "*Yif me my deeth, er*

---

[12] Livy, *The Early History of Rome*, trans. Aubrey de Selincourt (New York: Penguin Books, 1960), III.44–51.

[13] Gower's telling retains the suitor.

that I have a shame" (VI.249).[14]
In other words, she was asking for it.

The woman's "yes" to her own destruction resonates. Six centuries later, a meek lady of letters pens a text to amuse her lover and becomes the first female pornographer of record. O is one enormous yes, and she turns V's old yes on its ass with an actual request for death in the second ending of Histoire D'O. *The text implies a resurrection of both endings from an act of omission and silencing at the hands of a "suppressing" outside party or by the author herself:*

> *In a final chapter, which has been suppressed, O returned to Roissy, where she was abandoned by Sir Stephen.*
> *There exists a second ending to the story of O, according to which O, seeing that Sir Stephen was about to leave her, said she would prefer to die. Sir Stephen gave her his consent.*[15]

Thus an act of textual erasure (to keep the main character alive) becomes an act of textual revision that kills her.

Not only is V stripped of her original suitor, but her quest for secular learning (in Livy) is transformed into a spiritual errand through Chaucer's insertion of the temple. Centuries

---

[14] All citations of Chaucer's *Physician's Tale* from Larry D. Benson, gen. ed, *The Riverside Chaucer*, 3rd edn. (Boston: Houghton Mifflin, 1987), by fragment and line number.

[15] Fifteen years after the publication of *Histoire D'O*, Susan Sontag insisted that the heroine, O, remains sovereign, an assertion supported by the few — but pivotal — moments in the book when O is offered her freedom. In her essay entitled "The Pornographic Imagination," Sontag wrote, "That she chooses to die is O's ultimate choice, it is within her power. . . . Her condition . . . should not be understood as a by-product of her enslavement . . . but as the point of her situation, something she seeks and eventually attains": "The Pornographic Imagination," in Susan Sontag, *Styles of Radical Will* (New York: Farrar, Straus, and Giroux, 1969) 55 [35–73].

later, O, too, is stripped of ordinary social status and identity at the beginning of her story, removed from normal life while on an outing. She is also seized by a trusted figure — her own lover. Ordered into a car and told to ritualistically strip off her undergarments while remaining publicly dressed, she is relieved of her handbag, which the author notes contains all her identification papers. But she is not stripped of agency, albeit an agency expressed in abjection, submission, and abdication of self-sovereignty that leads directly to a transcendent state:

> *He began by saying that she should not think that she was now free. With one exception, and that was that she was free not to love him any longer, and to leave him immediately. But if she did love him, then she was in no wise free. She listened to him without saying a word, thinking how happy she was that he wanted to prove to himself — it mattered little how — that she belonged to him, and thinking too that he was more than a little naive not to realize that this proprietorship was beyond any proof. . . . The word "open" and the expression "opening her legs" were, on her lover's lips, charged with such uneasiness and power that she could never hear them without experiencing a kind of internal prostration, a sacred submission, as though a god, and not he, had spoken to her.[16]*

Thus begins her transfiguration through obloquy and eventual obliteration. By her own consent.

§ "SHE LISTENED TO HIM WITHOUT SAYING A WORD": OUI, NO, AND O

All the writers of the Virginia story face a dramatic difficulty in making the girl accessible after the trial so her father can

---

[16] Réage, *Story of O,* 54–55.

handily kill her. In Livy the father seizes the girl and dispatches her life in a public place (semi-public, actually, and foully ironic: her father takes her to an alley near the sheds of learning where all the trouble began). In Chaucer, the murder takes place at home: *He gooth hym hoom, and sette him in his halle, / And leet anon his deere doghter calle* (VI.207–208).

How does one verify the fact of a fable? The girl was never released, or she was never imprisoned. The yard was filled with the shards of her discarded toys, and the shit of the greyhounds her father kept; it was in Rome, or in Paris, or nowhere in between. *"There was nothing real about this country, which night had turned into make-believe, nothing except the smell of sage and lavender."*[17]

Centuries passed. Her father took her back to the sheds of learning. He took her directly from the courthouse, or he took her the next morning, on his way back. Or he took her behind the house, or in some anonymous alley that is the same in every city, in every city where an older man who claims rights to a younger woman will take her when he wants to do something unspeakable, in the name of love. *"There is only one way, my child, to make you free."*[18] Gently, with the lightest touch befitting a father whose daughter denies him nothing, he pushed her to her knees in the alley by the Forum, or in the yard where she'd once played, or in a place they'd never been. There, within sight of the temple where her prayers had once gone up to the goddess of wisdom, within sight of the apple tree she'd climbed and straddled, within shouting distance of the court of law, the first mid-morning rays of summer raised the stench of kitchen heaps and the indistinct odor of rats' tunnels, spilled wine, urine, and dust to her nostrils. She did nothing to resist. Did he ask her permission? They were alone. Who knows. He struck her a blow across the throat, and then no more. . . . *her refuge of*

---

[17] Réage, *Story of O,* 196.
[18] Livy, *The Early History of Rome,* 236.

silence.[19]

Chaucer didn't like this silence. Chaucer couldn't abide it. Chaucer elided the moment as best he could, made it better, made it worse:

"O gemme of chastitee, in pacience / Take thou thy deeth, for this is my sentence:/For love and nat for hate thou / most be deed; / My pitous hand moott smyten of thyn heed" (VI.223–226).

And she, silent so long, spoke her last: *one day this girl of whom I am speaking, and rightly so, since if I have nothing of hers she has everything of mine, the voice to begin with,*[20] "Blissed be God that I shal dye a mayde! / Yif me my deeth, er that I have a shame; / Dooth with youre child youre wyl, a Goddes name!" (VI.248–250).

The death is told with bloodless precision in ten one-syllable words. Except that Chaucer can't resist evoking the grim image of the Knight yanking his daughter's severed head up by the hair and tossing it at the feet of the corrupted Appius in open court. A sick joke: *Maidenhead is yours; just not the business end.*

A woman's consent to the impossible — the unthinkable, the inhumane and inhuman — has been a feature of stories of all sorts: the bestial transgressions of "Beauty and the Beast" and "The Frog Prince" (in which, in the unsanitized version, it is not a kiss that resurrects the prince to humanity but the princess's brutal act of frustration in throwing him against a wall, splitting his skin). "The Physician's Tale" and the *Story of*

---

[19] Réage, *Story of O*, 43.
[20] Réage, *Return to the Chateau*, 6.

O continue this night work.

In Chaucer's time, the fantasy of the all-encompassing female YES had a double in the knight's unwavering dedication to his lady and his state. The father Virginius has sworn allegiance to serve and submit to Appius, who is both judge and governor. The father's NO, paired with the girl's YES, cancels secular power over family, over purity, over sanctities and personal sovereignty. The father Virginius and the girl Virginia — in name practically one person, intimates of one another in the same way that God the Father and Jesus the Son are aspects of the same triadic identity, with the Holy Spirit being *wholly hole-y holy* in Its abundantly present Absence — are in a collusion of apostatic resistance, opting out of the formal judicial decision to which they are both bound for different reasons. He says he is freeing her. He is. He is not.

The woman who says yes to what is not possible and the knight who can save her from anything by doing what he likes to her — by carrying her away from the tower, by raping her in the form of a beast or a frog or a swan, by dropping her coffin and dislodging the stifling apple from her fallen throat, by killing her to save her honor — are central figures of the ourobourosian, slipping realities of these stories, what Andrea Dworkin calls the "double-double think" in her critique of *Histoire d'O:* "Everything is what it is, what it isn't, and its direct opposite."[21] As in the ancient wedding rites, in which a woman's silence represented consent, nothingness means everything. And it is the implicit power of NO — every woman's right even when trampled and unobserved — that makes the assent so tantalizing, whether by silence or by explicit statement. These moments in our stories take place beyond utterance, in paroxysmic union of Us with Other, in the dissolution of self in the annihilation of All:

---

[21] Andrea Dworkin, *Woman Hating* (New York: Plume, 1974).

Thus he would possess her as a god possesses his creatures, whom he lays hold of in the guise of a monster or a bird, of an invisible spirit or a state of ecstasy.[22]

In 1380, a curious legal proceeding concerning Geoffrey Chaucer came to light, hovered for a few months, then submerged into history's confusions without further explanation. On May 1 of that year, a woman named Cecily Champain agreed in a formal document to release Geoffrey Chaucer from responsibility for *omnimodas acciones tam de raptu meo* — any and all actions concerning her rape.[23] Two months later, two men named Richard Goodchild and John Grove issued the same sort of document releasing Chaucer from obligation for any harm done to them — no mention of rape. The same day, Cecily Champain "signed a nearly identical document releasing the same two men."[24] Three days later, John Grove paid Cecily Champain ten pounds.

We know less of this woman than we do of Chaucer himself. We know that she was fatherless, but not a minor — her father had died twenty-one years before. Her stepmother was likely Alice Perrers, mistress to the king and a close friend to Chaucer.[25] Was Cecily also a noted beauty, available and valuable as a commodity of pleasure? Had she given herself and regretted it, been taken by force, or perhaps been the bespoke property of another man, and fallen into or chosen the hands of another, or others? In any case, these documents acknowledge at least the aborted presence of an accusation of either rape or kidnapping, and it seems that a sum of money changed hands as recompense. And other men were involved

Although his work on the *Canterbury Tales* had its roots in

---

[22] Réage, *Story of O*, 31.

[23] Donald R. Howard, *Chaucer: His Life, His Works, His World* (New York: Ballantine Books, 1989), 317.

[24] Howard, *Chaucer*, 319.

[25] Howard, *Chaucer*, 318.

earlier work, it is generally agreed that Chaucer began the project in earnest after 1380. Important surveys have been made of the Tales' repeated references to rape, the coercion of women, and "the many different ways social structures are disrupted and redefined when women speak, specifically when they say yes and no."[26] If — and it is a rather large if — Chaucer had himself been redeemed after the rape of a woman, what demons might these tales have released and laid to rest for him?

To make up a story is a curious trap.[27]

In 1954 a shocking text surfaced in Paris. In just under 200 pages of cool, sinuous prose, it told the story of a young woman's induction into a life of bondage and submission. The scandal of the text was not that it was pornographic, but that its publisher claimed it was written by a woman. The first French edition carried a preface by prominent editor and taste-maker Jean Paulhan, who admired the book's "always pure and violent spirit, endless and unadulterated."[28]

The author would wait 40 years to speak up and claim the book. But Paulhan knew who she was: his adulterous companion for at least 8 years by then, and the only woman within the inner circle of men at Editions Gallimard. Quiet, unassuming, known for her demure and modest dress ("very pretty, in soft colors," one contemporary described her[29]*), Dominique Aury (itself a pseudonym, her given name at birth being Anne Declos) had nonetheless produced this lacerating work on a dare, because Paulhan believed no woman could write pornography. She balanced the book's entire existence on one irresistible conceit: The Woman Who Never Says No.*

"I advance through O with a strange feeling," said Paulhan, "as though I am moving through a fairy tale — we know that

---

[26] Elizabeth Robertson. "Comprehending Rape in Medieval England," *Medieval Feminists Forum* 21.1 (1996): 13–15.

[27] Réage, *Return to the Chateau,* 19.

[28] Réage, *Story of O,* xxiv.

[29] Quoted in *Writer of O,* dir. Pola Rapaport (Zeitgeist Films, 2006).

fairy tales are erotic novels for children."[30]

The book is hypnotic and seamless in the first sixty pages, spotty and hit-or-miss thereafter. It begins and ends abruptly, and twice each time. Ourobouros. The final word of the book, "consent," leaves the narrative hanging in the balance, at the point just after a verdict is rendered, yet before it is enacted.

Hire beautee was hire deth, I dar wel sayn.[31]

---

[30] Réage, *Story of O,* xxiii.
[31] Chaucer, *Physician's Tale,* VI.297.

⊖ Disconsolate Art

Myra Seaman

> The tomb is not a passage; it is a non-site that shelters an
> absence.
> ~Jean-Luc Nancy, *Dis-Enclosure: The Deconstruction
> of Christianity*

Art without consolation would, it seems, be fatally deficient.
Art's distinctive identity, central to a humanist aesthetic,
emanates from its supposedly singular capacity to transcend:
where humanists are menaced by meaninglessness, art offers
significance; where humanists lament loss, art reveals timeless
truth and enduring beauty; where humanists sense absence,
art promises presence. Humanist art consoles the living about
the dead and the losses they signify. It affirms the extension of
(human) life into the realms of the lifeless. Read (as it
customarily is) with such expectations, Chaucer's *Book of the
Duchess* becomes an artistic experiment in which the death of
John of Gaunt's wife provides Chaucer the matter through
which to transcend the boundaries of human life and, in that
act, create art.

But not so fast. Humanist traditions prepare readers for
such a result, and yet this narrative continuously avoids
granting it. Instead, the poem actively "refuses to re-figure
loss as transcendence."[1] It requires that we proclaim, along
with its proverbially obtuse narrator, that "She is dead!"[2] and,

---

[1] Louise O. Fradenburg, "'Voice Memorial': Loss and Reparation in
Chaucer's Poetry," *Exemplaria* 2.1 (March 1990): 177 [169–202].
[2] Geoffrey Chaucer, *Book of the Duchess*, in *The Riverside Chaucer*,
3rd edn., gen. ed. Larry D. Benson (Boston: Houghton Mifflin, 1987),

in the process, it "insist[s] on the irreducibility of certain limits."[3] Absence, loss, and the threat of meaninglessness all endure. The poem's many irresolvable ambiguities — its narrator's mysterious and unnatural illness, its melancholic modifications that transform Ovid's story of Ceyx (for Chaucer, Seys) and Alcyone into tragedy, its hyperbolic miscommunication between grieving knight and inquisitive dreamer — linger. In deliberately refusing transformation or transcendence, the poem enacts what I would call a disconsolate poetics, in which pain and suffering perdure, in which darkness obscures the light.

Within the narrative of the *Book of the Duchess*, the common expectation of transcendence through art is revealed in triplicate. Humanist readers abound. The narrator, afflicted with an undiagnosed illness one symptom of which is insomnia, turns to fictional art for comfort. Similarly, within the story to which the narrator turns to end his sleeplessness, art is once again expected to relieve suffering: here, artistry (in the form of the god Morpheus' performance of the dead Seys' persona while inhabiting his corpse) is expected to provide answers, to end pain through providing knowledge, to console by "soothing the pain, . . . retrieving the presence and the life of those who are dead."[4] This gesture of the faithful is echoed within the narrator's dream (itself generated by his reading) by a mysterious Man in Black who the narrator overhears expressing his grief over the loss of his beloved wife, Blanche (that is, 'White'), through lyric art. Yet in all three cases, and wholly contrary to the faith expressed by the three characters in their different narrative environments, calling on art to soothe, restore, and retrieve instead betrays an art whose power is limited and perhaps even fatal.

---

l. 1309 [pp. 329–346]. All further citations from this poem will be indicated, by line numbers, within the text.

[3] Fradenburg, "Voice Memorial," 177.

[4] Jean-Luc Nancy, *Dis-Enclosure: The Deconstruction of Christianity*, trans. Bettina Bergo, Gabriel Malenfant, and Michael B. Smith (New York: Fordham University Press, 2008), 99.

The experiences of the narrator and of the Man in Black imply this limitation: the narrator's reading increases rather than relieves his sorrow, while the Man in Black's poetic lament offers him no hope, not even the hope of communicating meaningfully with his living audience. The modified Ovidian story of Alcyone embodies this limitation directly and fully, leaving little doubt that faith in art as a tool for transcendence is misplaced. Indeed, the story-within-the-story bears no witness to Ovid's artistic transformation of tragedy into comedy, of death into (after)life, through the couple's transformation into birds. Instead, here, there is only death. When the corpse of Seys, artificially enlivened by Morpheus, appears at the bedside of a desperately anxious Alcyone to announce to her the details of his death, her own death is precipitated. The death of one causes the death of the other, through dashed hope of life after death. Chaucer focuses not on the metaphysical transcendence through transform-ation familiar from Ovid's version but instead on the mechanical animation of Seys, a unique feature of this version, which depends upon Morpheus' artistry. The dead Seys only appears to be alive — for humanist art convinces us of presence despite absence. Yet this simulation, in calling attention to its being *only* a simulation, reveals that art cannot create what is not but instead can only adapt what is. In her instructions to Morpheus (via her messenger), Juno says, "[T]ake up Seys body the king" (142); this body, referred to only as "hit," and not "he," is never (re)made into the king but can be only merely the semblance of him — made to speak "[r]ight as hit was wont to do, / The whyles that hit was on lyve" (149–150). This corpse is a lifeless object, albeit one that can be made to appear a still-living, still-human object, through the extreme verisimilitude of Morpheus' artistry.

This art, however, does not provide the desired presence but instead emphasizes the feared absence. It affirms for Alcyone the aptness of her grieving. She who was once "[t]he beste that mighte bere lyf" (64) is transformed by the news to the epitome of the unliving, the inorganic: twice she "fil a-swown as cold as ston" (123, 126–127). The knowledge she sought induces her own death, a death that is an extension of her suspended living: she has, for days prior to the nighttime vision, been just this side of death, due to her inability to eat and her general lack of investment in life. Her appearing dead though still alive is contrasted utterly by the animation of her dead lover, which puts her in league with the inhabitants of the timeless world of the Cave of Sleep from which Morpheus has been briefly roused. Morpheus' temporary illusory transform-ation of Seys' lifeless body offers, instead of transcendence, only a vivid reminder of what has been irretrievably lost. Everything Seys requests, as he appears to Alycone, including his own burial and the reduction of her sorrow, assuring her that "I nam but ded" (304), apparently is for nought: She dies in three days. Like Alcyone, like Seys, we receive no consolation. The reanimation of Seys' lifeless body, through Morpheus' art, produces only death.

The Man in Black attempts through his verse something similar to Morpheus' animation, the "revivification of the dead White, . . . reading the past into the present and the present into the past."[5] Painfully, though, the poem repeatedly raises this hope while only leaving it deferred. The dreamer is himself suspended between life and death, with "felyng in nothing" and sensing only that "Al is ylyche god to me" (11, 9). He wonders, as a result, "How that I live" (2), for "wel ye woot, agaynes kynde / Hit were to liven in this wyse" (16–17). He turns to narrative to alleviate his mysterious affliction but finds there instead a double-death. This failure of art-as-remedy is then followed by his encounter with the Man in Black's loss, a loss that the dreamer refuses to accept until the Man in Black can stand it no longer. The dreamer is not attached to Blanche individually, like Alcyone is to Seys and the Man in Black is to his queen, so his resistance to acknowledging intense loss is because, as the dreamer proclaims in horror, "Is that your los? By god, hit is routhe!"

---

[5] Nancy Ciccone, "The Chamber, the Man in Black, and the Structure of Chaucer's Book of the Duchess," *The Chaucer Review* 44.2 (2009): 208 [205–23].

(1310). From art, then, the narrator gained "swich pite and swich routhe / To rede hir sorwe, that, by my trouthe, / I ferde the worse al the morwe" (97–99). The series of encounters with art amounts to a series of encounters with death, with sorrow untranscended. The bleakness of Alcyone's experience of loss — a loss re-enacted for her through Juno's art — places all that follows in the poem in a shadow that is never eradicated, despite repeated expectation by those who suffer loss that art will produce precisely that transformation.

While Seys' reanimated body becomes a tool of destruction, killing his wife's hopes and thereby killing her, another Ovidian figure of transformation and transcendence becomes, through a certain Middle English disconsolate poetics, a self-destructive rejection of love's, and art's, capacity to move us beyond the limitations of earthly existence — of life. In the anonymous fourteenth-century Middle English romance *Sir Orfeo*, a lively adaptation of Ovid's Orpheus and Eurydice story, it is a husband suffering the loss of his wife who physically and spiritually removes himself from human community, entering a deathlike state while experiencing the loss of — and with little hope for the return of — the absent beloved. His actions thus mirror those of Alcyone in the dreamer's book in Chaucer's *Book of the Duchess*. Seys and Heurodys are both tangibly alive, through the vividness of the poetic representation of their vulnerable bodies, and yet they are both in that precise moment absent, literally beyond human life.

In this case, the Fairy King abducts Heurodys (alternatively, Meurodys in the version of *Orfeo* as it appears in Manuscript Ashmole 61), and while she is ultimately retrieved from her imprisonment in the fairy kingdom, she is nearly immediately dead (again). The artistry of the poem, in fact, lingers (twice) on her self-mutilation and on her suspension in a living death. First, when she obeys the Fairy King's demand that she submit to him, Heurodys is palpably present as she tears at her body, shredding her skin and making us feel her physicality, as does Orfeo who describes her actions to her, in her distant madness:

> Thy flessch that was so whyte beforn
> With thi nayles thou hast torn.
> Thy lyppes that were so bryght rede
> Semys as wan as thou were dede.
> And thi fyngyrs long and smale,
> Thei be blody and all pale.[6]

And yet at this moment she is somewhere beyond human life, mentally and emotionally elsewhere as she anticipates transference to the inhuman fairy kingdom.

Death in *Orfeo* masquerades as fairy abduction. Heurodys has literally been taken by the Fairy King from this world to another, at a pre-arranged time. Yet the effects of his intervention are precisely those effects known to be the result of death: after Heurodys tears at her body to the point that Orfeo says she appears dead she explains that they simply must part, despite their great love and harmonious life. This is a deathbed scene (100), with Orfeo's response expressing precisely our questions at the moment of death — like Orfeo, we often ask of the departing beloved, "Where are you going?" and "Why can't I go with you?" When she recounts what the fairy king requires of her, it's as if she is being taken to heaven — confirmed later in the poem, in the Auchinleck manuscript's version of *Orfeo*, when Orfeo enters the Fairy King's castle and perceives it as "Paradise"[7] — and if she resists, she will experience the physical torments generally associated with hell (175). These are the proverbial choices of death. Later, Orfeo enters the Fairy King's hall and is told that none has ever entered without first being requested — that is, required — to come. No one, but Orfeo, chooses death.

---

[6] Anonymous, *Sir Orfeo*, in *Codex Ashmole 61: A Compilation of Popular Middle English Verse*, ed. George Shuffelton (Kalamazoo: Medieval Institute Publications, 2008), ll. 95–96 [pp. 386–99]. All following citations from this poem will be indicated, by line numbers, within the text.

[7] Anonymous, *Sir Orfeo*, in *The Middle English Breton Lays*, ed. Anne Laskaya and Eve Salisbury (Kalamazoo: Medieval Institute Publications, 1995), l. 376.

Orfeo's sorrow at his beloved's departure is put in terms of his wanting to die, of having lived too long. When given the chance, upon seeing her a decade later, he promptly follows her, as if to his own end. Indeed, upon his return to Winchester/Thrace later, an incognito Orfeo tells a story to his former steward about King Orfeo's supposed death, which is expressed in terms of his having been torn to pieces by lions, paralleling what his wife did to herself before her departure from the land of the living (528). Both Orfeo and Heurodys have experienced a death through dismemberment made possible only through art.

The enforced transformation of the effectively-dead in *Sir Orfeo* is performed by another supernatural artist, this time the Fairy King playing the role of Chaucer's Morpheus in his manipulation of Heurodys' body, which upon its abduction is no longer her own. Her permanent suspension between life and death is observed, ten years after she has been taken to the Fairy Kingdom, by Orfeo when he follows her to the castle of the Fairy King, presents himself to the porter as a minstrel, and is led to the King via a hall where he observes the following:

> Than lokyd he aboute the walle,
> And saw it stond over alle
> With men that were thyder brought,
> And semyd dede and were nought.
> Som ther stod withoutyn hede,
> And some armys non hade,
> And som ther bodys had wounde
> And som onne hors ther armyd sette,
> And som were strangyld at ther mete
> And men that were nomen wyth them ete;
> So he saw them stonding ther.
> Than saw he men and women in fere
> As thei slepyd ther undryntyde;
> He them saw on every syde.
> Among them he saw hys wyve
> That he lovyd as hys lyve,

> That ley ther under that tre full trew;
> Be hyr clothys he hyr knew. (378–395)

Orfeo's encounter with his wife's suspended animation recalls Seys' nighttime appearance to Alcyone; in this case, the Fairy King's abductees — among them Orfeo's wife Heurodys whom he has transformed into a work of art — are trapped in their moment of abduction in a kind of grotesque tableau. Both poems turn hopefully to art but find it infused with death rather than sustaining life. Orfeo's art, functionally competing against the Fairy King's art in a sort of Battle of the Bands, is his tool in a rescue fantasy that, as Fradenburg explains via Freud in "A Special Type of Choice of Object Made by Men," is a "renegotiatio[n] of mortality: the fantasy is that if we can save someone, we might perhaps have power over life and death."[8]

During the preceding decade in the wilderness, Orfeo has lived among the animals and used his art, his harping, as an artistic expression that had the opposite effect of the Man in Black's lament of his own spousal loss, for Orfeo "temperyd hys herpe with a mery soune, / And harpyd after hys wane wylle" (274–275). Art is for Orfeo distraction from, rather than expression of, sorrow. The effect is that "The wyld bestys that ther were, / They com aboute hys harpe to here . . . meke and myld" (277–280). When he is harping is also when fairies are closest, when Orfeo can see their courtly excursions for hawking and hunting. Art thus seems to be associated with stillness and also with that which is beyond life, at the edges of life (285 ff.). Art's association with peril is highlighted by the way the "strange, troubled catalogue of the undead is a catalogue of stories, trapped in the library of the fairy king."[9]

---

8 Louise O. Fradenburg, "'Fulfild of fairye': The Social Meaning of Fantasy in the *Wife of Bath's Prologue* and *Tale*," in Peter G. Beidler, ed., *Geoffrey Chaucer: Wife of Bath (Case Studies in Contemporary Criticism)* (Boston: Bedford Books, 1996), 210 [205–220].

9 Ellen M. Caldwell, "The Heroism of Heurodis: Self-Mutilation and Restoration in *Sir Orfeo*," *Papers on Language & Literature* [*PLL*]

The poem, like *Book of the Duchess*, reveals through this horrific image — emphasized in the poetic repetitions of art and suffering seen in this passage — art's tendency to trap and fix, rather than to release and revive.

In these two poems, artistry is deployed to make the bodies of those who have been lost endure. In the classic William Hope Hodgson horror novel *The Night Land*, Eugene Thacker sees a tension between life and the human that applies to Seys' artificial reappearance and to Heurodys' appearance in the weird tableau: "unable to distinguish the living from the nonliving . . . everything appears to be alive, but none of it is alive in any naturalistic, let alone humanistic, sense of the term."[10] The contemporary equivalent would be the sus-pended animation of the zombie. Morpheus, not Seys, inhabits his body and speaks words of love to his wife, an imposter. The true horror of Heurodys' dreamy courtly outings into the earthly forest, where she cannot speak and can only peer out from her physical shell and eventually recognize her husband, are witnessed by Orfeo when he enters the Fairy castle and sees her permanently bound in her moment of abduction. These two scenarios offer specimens of medieval supernatural horror, presenting — as Thacker says modern supernatural horror does — "a furtive, miasmatic unintelligibility that inhabits any ontology of life: the idea of a 'life' that is not simply an anthropomorphic, human-centric idea of life." The life witnessed here looks more like death, and yet is indiscernible from what we know of life. What results is "a concept of life that is itself, in some basic way, unhuman, a life without us."[11] Both scenes affirm Thacker's observation

---

43.3 (2007): 305–306 [291–310].

[10] Eugene Thacker, *After Life* (Chicago: University of Chicago Press, 2010), 267–268. See also E. R. Truitt, who analyzes the appearance of tomb automata in medieval literary texts in order to trace a range of "inorganic, artificial, magical objects [that] confound the simplistic binary of 'life' and 'death' by obscuring the boundaries between them, and by embodying a third category" ("Fictions of Life and Death," *postmedieval* 1.1/2 [2010]: 197 [194–98]).

[11] Thacker, *After Life*, 268.

that "[w]hile human beings or human groups are obviously involved in such events, there is also a sense in which such events are beyond human comprehension." For the duration of these experiences, with Orfeo and Alcyone we observe, even as with the dreamer of the *Book of the Duchess* we resist acknowledging, that "life is human-centered and yet un-human-oriented."[12]

Disconsolate art not only fails to console but refuses. In the process, it even rubs our faces in it, for the only transcendence presented in these poems is literal, not metaphysical. Seys hovers over Alcyone's bed, in a dream but very real (literally, figurally textualized), completely present but simultaneously absent; Heurodys is already in the Fairy Kingdom as she tries to remove her earthly human body as if to escape to the fate she has not chosen but must take on, and then becomes part of an atemporal tableau of suffering even as she also inhabits the Fairy world and enters at times into the human realm. These lingering loci of darkness are central moments in two poems of lamentation that hypothesize art as a means of consolation. Each scene is one of endless depth, of timeless suspension, of unease, in a narrative interrogating the capacity of art to transcend — or at least disregard — such moments of recognition, in support of life. In *Sir Orfeo*, the music of Orfeo's harp turns even wild animals still; in *Book of the Duchess*, poetry holds transcendent potential. Yet all fail to provide a panacea. Orfeo's harping can't prevent the removal of his beloved from earthly living and can't return her there, either; its effects on the animals, stilling the active vitality within them, hint instead at art's deadly potential. Heurodys' husband tells her to "late be all this reufull crye" (102), just as, in Chaucer's narrative, Alcyone's encourages her to "Let be your sorwful lyf" (202), but the only way either can do this is through death. Orfeo's response is to stop living: since he can't quite kill himself literally, he kills his persona as king and as a member of the community and encourages in his mourning subjects the same recognition and acceptance

---

[12] Thacker, *After Life*, ix.

Heurodys encouraged in him upon her departure: "Do wey . . . it schall be so" (228).

The living are urged by the dead to let them go, an impossible demand which is met instead with the griever's departure from society and loss of individual identity, with each trapped in a *locus amoenus* become loathsome dream-scape. This death calls for the "adieu" that, as Jean-Luc Nancy recounts, Derrida in a collection of memorial addresses (*Each Time Unique, the End of the World*), claimed "should salute nothing other than 'the necessity of a possible non-return, the end of the world as the end of any resurrection'" so that it is a "definitive leave-taking, an irremissible abandonment — as much an abandonment of the deceased other to his effacement as an abandonment of the survivor to the rigorous privation of all hope in some kind of afterlife."[13] With Derrida, Nancy explains that, "We must say 'adieu' without return, in the implacable certainty that the other will not turn back, will never return."[14] Death, not Life, is human acceptance of the impossibility of producing a desired effect, a "letting be." Only because he lacks true understanding can the dreamer-narrator of *Book of the Duchess* wake from his dream. The Man in Black and Alcyone are trapped (in art) by their own recognition. Art promises relief from suffering but instead serves only to remind us that living is suffering, a death in life. Art offers us, like the figures throughout these two narratives, more reason to tremble than to rest — a disconsolate art.

---

[13] Nancy, *Dis-Enclosure*, 98. See also Jacques Derrida, *Chaque Fois Unique, La Fin du Monde*, ed. Pascale-Anne Brault and Michael Naas (Paris: Éditions Galilée, 2003).

[14] Nancy, *Dis-Enclosure*, 99.

✸ Kill Me, Save Me, Let Me Go
Custance, Virginia, Emelye

Karl Steel

The inevitability of bad *Fama* worries a few of Chaucer's heroines. Cresseid and Dido prefer that their shame not be spread about, while the Wife of Bath prefers to seize the means of narrative production.[1] Each worries about what will be said about her; each justifies her actions; but none recognizes that, as a literary character, she could not have done other than she did.

This is where Custance, Virginia, and Emelye differ. It is the difference between saying, "I wish you wouldn't talk about me this way" and saying, instead, "why are you doing this to me?" or, more precisely, "Why are you making me do this?" For each one knows, if only for a moment, that the responsibility for what happens to her and through her lies elsewhere. Each experiences the precise opposite of self-awareness, for each momentarily struggles against the narrative before realizing herself to be *not* a self but rather someone else's creature, destined to be rewarded or to suffer regardless of what she does, destined to be made to be satisfied with what happens, destined to be exemplary whether she wants to or not, because she comes to know that

---

[1] See for example J. Stephen Russell, "Dido, Emily, and Constance: Femininity and Subversion in the Mature Chaucer," *Medieval Perspectives* 1 (1988, for 1986): 66 [65–74]: "Dido is a woman incarcerated in the epic world of the *Aenied*."

her wants are not her own. At once constituted and dispossessed by her tale, each implicitly repeats one of Žižek's favorite maxims, Deleuze's "si vous êtes pris dans le rêve de l'autre, vous êtes foutu"[2] ["if you're caught in the dream of another, you're fucked"]. One seeks death; another wants to be something other than a creature of her father; and the last tries to exempt herself from the tale's political reconciliation. None gets what she wants: one forced to live, one to die, one to love, each gets just enough awareness of being in their stories to know that they want out. Then the door slams shut.

§ CUSTANCE

When a ship wrecks on the Northumbrian coast, a constable from a nearby castle scavenges it, and finds, amid the treasure, Custance. After a fashion, she begs to be freed from suffering:

> In hir langage mercy she bisoghte.
> The lyf out of hire body for to twynne,
> Hire to deliver of wo that she was inne (II.516–518)[3]

In a scene unique to Chaucer's version of the story,[4] Custance begs for death, partially in "a maner Latyn corrupt" (II.519), and partially, one must imagine, with gestures. Her motives are unclear, though if she thinks death mercy, then she must

---

[2] For example, *Violence: Six Sideways Reflections* (New York: Picador, 2008), 57. For the maxim's source (ultimately in a 1987 lecture, "Qu'est-ce que l'acte de création"), see Gilles Deleuze, *Deux Régimes de Fous, textes et entretiens 1975-1995*, ed. David Lapoujade (Paris: Minuit, 2003), 297; translation mine.

[3] All citations of Chaucer's *Canterbury Tales* from *The Riverside Chaucer*, gen. ed. Larry D. Benson, 3rd edn. (Oxford: Oxford University Press, 1987), by fragment and line number.

[4] Robert M. Correale, "The Man of Law's Prologue and Tale," in *Sources and Analogues of the Canterbury Tales*, ed. Robert M. Correale and Mary Hamel, 2 Vols. (Woodbridge, Suffolk: Boydell and Brewer, 2006), 302–303, 332–333 [277–350].

be suffering terribly from being passed from one man to another.

Her death would interrupt this commerce. It would save her from another marriage, and save her, ultimately, from being returned to her Roman father, who, the Man of Law too earnestly assures us, lacks any incestuous desires. It would save her from continuing to be presented as a sanctified, perfectly submissive wife and daughter. She seeks death to exempt herself from this airtight exemplary narrative, for it is not just death she wants, but death for no clear reason. She wants it from someone who knows nothing of her, who wants nothing from her. The motiveless killing she seeks would grant her a *senseless* end, one that could not be interpreted within the constraints of the tale. The death she wants would be an event, an action from nowhere in the system as currently constituted, opening the sacrificial logic of female thralldom (II.286–87) to the otherwise unthinkable.[5]

Then the moment passes. In one of the very few critical assessments of her request, Kolve characterizes Custance as "experienc[ing] and express[ing] total despair," from which "she soon recovers herself."[6] Kolve takes Constance as feeling something, and then deciding to feel something else more authentically in line with her true, holy self. He ends his attention to her despair as quickly as the tale itself does. But if we take the interruption of the despair seriously, if we stop the tale for a time to linger in it, we can watch Constance seeking an escape, and then see that escape taken from her. She is

---

[5] I have Alain Badiou in mind. For a helpful explanation, see Christopher Norris: "events" are "those strictly unforeseeable and — as they appear at the time in question — wholly contingent irruptions of the new that may turn out to exert a uniquely powerful and lasting effect but which elude ontological specification precisely insofar as they belong to no existing (i.e. up-to-now thinkable) order of things" (*Badiou's Being and Event: A Reader's Guide* [London: Continuum, 2009], 9).

[6] V. A. Kolve, *Chaucer and Imagery of Narrative: The First Five Canterbury Tales* (Stanford: Stanford University Press, 1984), 303.

made to go on to show herself cleansed of despair by serving in the constable's household "withouten slouthe" (II.530), which is to say, without the *acedia* that might lead her once again to seek death.[7] In short, the tale gives Constance a brief moment in which she might have escaped, and then compels her to be happy on its terms.[8] Had she persisted in her unhappiness, had she refused to persist in her love for the beautiful and saintly body that so many others desire, had she, in short, ceased her constancy, who knows what would have happened? Perhaps nothing, in the sense that the narrative would have ended, or that the narrative that had been told after her death would be illegible within the legendary logic in which Custance suffers. This would have been a story ended by its subject's life now "twynned" from her body, a life now nowhere, or elsewhere in ways impossible for the tale to think.

§ VIRGINIA

In Livy and the *Roman de la Rose*, Chaucer's most proximate source for the *Physician's Tale*, Virginius, not his daughter, is the focus of a tale less about a thwarted sexual crime than about political corruption and revolution; Virginius kills his daughter precipitously, in public; and Virginia has no chance to protest — and then to consent to — her father's plan to behead her.[9] In Chaucer's wholly invented scene, the private,

---

[7] For an efficient treatment of *acedia* and a guide to its scholarship, see Gregory M. Sedlack, *Idleness Working: The Discourse of Love's Labor from Ovid through Chaucer and Gower* (Washington, D.C.: Catholic University of America, 2004), 171–174.

[8] For more on happiness and the status quo, see Sara Ahmed, *The Promise of Happiness* (Durham: Duke University Press, 2010).

[9] Kenneth Bleeth, "The Physician's Tale," *Sources and Analogues,* Vol. 2, 546 and 550 [535–564]. What follows is sympathetic to Michael Stugrin's characterization of the scene as one in which father and daughter experience an "overwhelming sense of helplessness to effect any change in what they both recognize as their approaching fate[,which] goes beyond the plot of the tale and its moral

bereaved colloquy between father and daughter, Virginia asks
for mercy (VI.231), begs for "grace" or a "remedye" (VI.236),
and asks for time:

> My deeth for to compleyne a litel space;
> For, pardee, Japte yaf his doghter grace
> For to compleyne er he hir slow, allas! (VI.239–241)

Then she faints, rises from her swoon to declare "Blissed be
God that I shal dye a mayde. / Yif me my deeth er that I have a
shame" (VI.248–249), and faints again. Then her father
beheads her.

The last decade's work on this scene has often tried to
determine why Virginia's resistance collapses.[10] Without
aiming to displace these readings, I offer an answer that could
not be more straightforward. Or circular. She consents to her
death because she has to die. She consents to patriarchal
authority, but, in a larger sense, she is consenting to the
inevitability of the tale itself. Note Chaucer's emphasis on the
tale's historicity. Its first line ascribes the events to "Titus
Livius" (VI.1); amid Apius's scheming, he assures us that "this
is no fable / But knowen for historial thyng notable" (VI.155–
156); and Virginia herself is like a book (VI.108), offered up as
an example in which "maydens myghten rede" (VI.107) what
the logic of virginity would make them do or suffer.

Working with the book of history, Chaucer cannot rescue
Virginia. He can just change Livy enough to give Virginia
space to try, and to fail, to save herself from her own story.

---

implication": "Ricardian Poetics and Late Medieval Cultural
Pluriformity: The Significance of Pathos in the *Canterbury Tales*,"
The Chaucer Review 15 (1980): 158 [155–167].

[10] For several good treatments, see Lianna Farber, "The Creation of
Consent in the *Physician's Tale*," *Chaucer Review* 39.2 (2004) 151–
164; Holly A. Crocker, *Chaucer's Visions of Manhood* (New York:
Palgrave, 2007), 51–76; and Daniel T. Kline, "Jephthah's Daughter
and Chaucer's Virginia: The Critique of Sacrifice in the *Physician's
Tale*," *Journal of English and Germanic Philology* 107 (2008) 77–103.

When Virginia compares herself to Jephthah's daughter, she necessarily freights this comparison with the standard exegesis, which almost universally condemns Jephthah for, at best, his foolishness and at worst for the obscenity of human sacrifice.[11] Wielding this exegesis through her comparison, she accuses her father and indeed the whole of the patriarchy of a bullheaded commitment to values that would better be abandoned. At the same time, she asks for a pause. During this time, had he granted it, her father might think rather than act. During this time out of time, or — more accurately — during this moment when time's stream becomes a floodplain that might empty in any direction, history's inevitability might cease, and something else might occur.

Her father does wait, a little. For the first time, Virginia faints, and her father does not act, not yet. It is a critical commonplace that Virginius thinks of his daughter as an aspect of himself; hence his otherwise ludicrous or contemptible lament, "O deere doughter, endere of my lyf" (VI.218). He might have continued to recognize her during her unconsciousness, and seen his own subjection to the historical narrative mirrored in his daughter's passivity. Instead he waits only for her to rise and to accept what will happen. The tale's exemplary logic requires that she come to long enough to agree to die, to prevent her death from being murder. Then the tale has her fall back into unconsciousness, unable to feel, unable to act, able only to be sacrificed. Virginia beheads her and goes out, thinking he has done right when all that he has done is to have done right by Livy's script.[12]

---

[11] Most recently, see Kline, "Critique of Sacrifice."

[12] In writing this paragraph, I have had in mind Žižek's reading of Melville's Bartleby the Scrivener as someone whose "gesture of pure withdrawal" refuses to perpetuate the dance of negation; see *The Parallax View* (Boston: MIT Press, 2006), 381–385. For a lucid exposition of these pages, see Jodi Dean, *Žižek's Politics* (New York: Routledge, 2006), 22–23, 130–131, 168–171, 197–199.

§ EMELYE

At first glance, she does not quite belong in this set. She does beg the goddess Diana to rescue her from the obligation to marry the tournament's victor, and thus she, like Custance and Virginia, resists the tale for a time. But Chaucer adopts this scene almost entirely intact from Boccaccio's *Teseida*; unlike the *Man of Law's* and *Physician's Tale*, he invents very little here.[13] In the *Knight's Tale*, Emelye reminds Diana of her devoted service to hunting; she alone of the tale's characters wants peace between Palemon and Arcite; and she arrives at the shrine with a throng of "hir maydens" (I.2275), as if dramatizing her preference for female company, and as if she had carved out a kind of Amazonian autonomous zone within patriarchal Athens; all these points hold true as well for Boccaccio's Emilia.

Chaucer's key change is in his heroine's willingness to play the role that she must. Despite her protests, Boccaccio's Emilia is open to love and hopes not so much to be rescued as to have Diana decide for her, since each one of her suitors pleases her equally ("tanto ciascun piacievole mi pare"[14]). Through Emelye's protests, strident and protracted, and her bitterness when she realizes Diana has forsaken her, Chaucer signals a far more dedicated Amazon than the one Boccaccio provided.

To this Chaucer adds the text's own resistance to Emelye's prayer. Most obviously, he ends the scene with "ther is namoore to seye" (I.2366), at once concluding both Emelye's hope and her voice. Once Emelye has had her say and found no response but that of the mechanistically advancing plot, she herself falls wordless. From here on out, she allows herself to be moved forward to meet the needs of the story, sloughing

---

[13] William E. Coleman, "The Knight's Tale," in *Sources and Analogues*, Vol. 2, 129 and 177–183 [87–248].

[14] *Teseida* VII.85, qtd. from Coleman, "The Knight's Tale," in *Sources and Analogues*, Vol. 2, 181.

off her indifference to her suitors by weeping with Palamon when it is required (I.2817), and proving in the end to be a perfect, loving wife (I.3103).[15] All that suggests Emelye's continued resistance is the enjambment at I.3105–3106, where Palamon serves her so nobly "that nevere was ther no word hem bitwene / Of jalousi or any oother teene." *No word hem bitwene*: for a moment, Chaucer allows a hint of the deadly silence of a match crafted not for love but for statecraft, concocted by a ruler unconcerned with canon law's insistence on the importance of consent in validating a marriage.[16] When the tale adds "thus ended Palamon and Emelye" (I.3107), we might pity these two, condemned to play out the fantasy of an impossible peace between Athens and Thebes and between Athens and the Amazons, each rescued from one death and defeat only to be dragooned into the living death of Theseus's utopia.

Emelye's compulsion runs still deeper than Theseus's machinations. Towards the end of the scene, Boccaccio has Emilia ask Diana whether the gods had already decided by an

---

[15] The second chapter of Angela Jane Weisl's *Conquering the Reign of Femeny: Gender and Genre in Chaucer's Romance* (Rochester: D. S. Brewer, 1995), which contrasts Emelye's "balked desire to opt out of the romance" (59) to Canacee's sabotage of the plot of the *Squire's Tale*, is very much in sympathy with my argument. For a compelling alternate reading of Emelye's inconsistent behavior (and Diana's otherwise inexplicable foreknowledge) as the tale's sign of both feminine difference and adventure itself, see Susan Crane, *Gender and Romance in Chaucer's Canterbury Tales* (Princeton: Princeton University Press, 1994), 173, 185.

[16] Elizabeth Robertson, "Marriage, Mutual Consent, and the Affirmation of the Female Subject in the *Knight's Tale*, the *Wife of Bath's Tale*, and the *Franklin's Tale*," in Wendy Harding, ed., *Drama, Narrative and Poetry in* The Canterbury Tales (Toulouse: Presses Universitaires du Mirail, 2003), 181–184 [175–193]. See also Elizabeth Fowler, "Chaucer's Hard Cases," in Barbara A. Hanawalt and David Wallace, eds., *Medieval Crime and Social Control* (Minneapolis: University of Minnesota Press, 1999), 136–137 [124–142].

eternal word ("con etterna parola")[17] that she must marry. Chaucer gives this line to the goddess herself, who proclaims that "among the goddes hye it is affermed, / And by eterne word writen and confermed" (I.2349–2350) that Emelye must marry. Emilia had asked a question, whereas Emelye gets an answer that, nonetheless, conceals from her precisely what will happen — no doubt in part because it hardly matters which suitor she marries.[18] Furthermore, the orality of the term *parola* allows for a kind of deliberation, or at least suggests a subjective divine fiat, as in the creation story of the first chapter of Genesis. It allows for a decision to have occurred and thus suggests that it might have gone otherwise. For this *parola*, Chaucer substitutes a written commandment that can only be affirmed by the gods, a *diktat* inscribed by whom or to what end no one knows. All that Emelye can know is that what will happen has already been written. She has been fated to love and to live on for the benefit of Theseus, for the Knight, for Chaucer himself. She has been condemned to this plot as soon as Theseus conquered the Amazons and future writers decided on the necessity of getting it correct.

§ CODA: THE MAN HIMSELF

The above may seem perverse given Chaucer's well-known freedom with his sources, particularly in these three tales. But his freedom could go only so far. Chaucer found his freedom in selecting his material, in rhetoric, trimming, pacing, and amplification, but he could not deny the larger logics of sanctity, political exemplarity, and romance. I present this chapter as an offering to the continuing conversations on Chaucer's interest in fate and free will, and also as an implicit

---

[17] *Teseida* VII.85, quoted from Coleman, "The Knight's Tale," in *Sources and Analogues,* Vol. 2, 181.

[18] I say this against the frequent and to my mind misguided attempts in the criticism to characterize Palamon as more moral or deserving of life than Arcite.

exploration of what is being required of us when scholarship demands our faithfulness to our sources and history, when it tells us that proper scholars must let the text decide. Finally, I suggest that Chaucer turned to female characters — these and others (Griselda most notably) — to think through his own passivity in relation to a textual history that allowed him to go only so far. Like so many writers, he makes his female characters suffer. But to some of these, he gave a brief awareness of what he was doing to them, or what various conjoined patriarchal logics and received narratives made him do. Perhaps in his darker moods, or during fits of self-pity, he felt himself trapped by his own materials, moved by them against his other wishes, and he found a mirror in women he made to live, to die, to marry, he and they caught up in systems that required their obedience without giving them any meaningful chance to say no.

The *Physician's Tale* as Hagioclasm

Elaine Treharne

Adroit scholarly interpretation of the *Physician's Tale* over the last half century has sought to rehabilitate what is perceived as one of Chaucer's least satisfactory tales. Arguments have focused on the correlation of teller and tale; Chaucer's manipulation of his sources; and the foregrounding of various key aspects of the tale, such as governance, virginity or the legal system. In seeking to round off the *Tale*, to give it cohesion and moral purpose, for example, Kirk L. Smith concludes his discussion about the judicial and medical elements with the opinion that "The tale offers this moral cure: abjuring the exploitation in which self-absorbed Apius indulges, the worthy practitioner would earn the public's esteem by pledging disinterested service."[1] Similarly, in Jerome Mandel's view, the careful structure of the *Tale* and its emphasis on death can be paralleled with *The Pardoner's Tale*, with which it is paired in Fragment VI.[2] Crafton's recent judicious appraisal focuses on shared concerns between the *Parson's Tale* and the *Physician's* created by the use of preaching motifs, the *Summa virtutem remediis anime* and the

---

[1] Kirk L. Smith, "False Care and the Canterbury Cure: Chaucer Treats the New Galen," *Literature & Medicine* 27 (2009): 71 [61–81].

[2] Jerome Mandel, *Geoffrey Chaucer, Building the Fragments of the "Canterbury Tales,"* (Madison, NJ: Fairleigh Dickinson University Press, 1972), 50–69, where, however, Mandel seems to imply that the *Physician's Tale* acts primarily as a foil for the Pardoner.

theme of "false virginity."[3] Other critics have highlighted the use of hagiographic topoi in the *Tale*. In Lee Patterson's clever and insightful *Chaucer and the Subject of History*, he judges the *Tale* as aspiring to "hagiographical authority," as a "quasi hagiography" in which the heroine, Virginia, is a "helpless victim," subordinated to her persecutors' narrative dominance.[4] "In short," states Patterson, the *Physician's Tale* "is a fraudulent or 'counterfeit' hagiography . . . unable to transcend its own fallen historicity."[5]

Patterson's illuminating reading of the *Physician's Tale* is used principally to introduce the longer discussion of the false language of the *Pardoner's Tale*, the work that has generally dominated discussion of this textual pair in Fragment VI. This brief essay will focus again on the *Physician's Tale* as a "quasi-hagiography," but in order to speculate upon Chaucer's deliberate critique of the prolific hagiographic genre in the medieval period. In the light of Chaucer's frequent tendency to play with audience expectations of genre and of literary convention, this contribution will read the *Tale* as a deliberate clinical dismemberment of generic convention and a provocative disembowelling of the corpus of virgin martyrs' passions.

§ MANIPULATING EXPECTATIONS: APPEARANCE AND REALITY

Much of Chaucer's *Canterbury Tales* functions as a dialogic text, demanding the interaction of the audience or reader. This writerly style is both engaging and challenging; ultimately, meaning inheres in the interpretative space between text and reception. If this were not the case, then

---

[3] John Michael Crafton, "'The cause of everiche maladye': A New Source of the *Physician's Tale*," *Philological Quarterly* 84 (2005): 259–285.

[4] Lee Patterson, *Chaucer and the Subject of History* (Madison: University of Wisconsin Press, 1991), 368–369.

[5] Patterson, *Chaucer and the Subject of History*, 370.

characters as diverse as the Knight or the Wife of Bath could not have elicited the very wide range of critical response that they have over the last six centuries. Similarly, Chaucer's manipulation of generic convention opens up his text to reader speculation and scholarly debate. Thus, the *Knight's Tale*, as a Romance, has the happy ending expected of the genre, but it is one profoundly overshadowed by the grimness of the gods and their temples, the objectification of Emelye, and the death of Arcite; the *Parson's Tale*, as a learned and pious sermon, ought to cure the soul, but instead, its sturdy prose and considerable length seem to doom it to literary and spiritual obscurity; and the *Reeve's Tale* has all the elements of the fabliau, but the verbal malevolence of its teller and the sinister implications of the Reeve's portrait mean that what should simply be bawdy becomes overtly disturbing.

In the case of the *Physician's Tale*, the formulae of hagiography are immediately apparent in the motifs introducing the female subject of the story, Virginia. She is described in terms familiar to virgin martyr narratives; that is, as an image only, a formula — one that typifies the Virgin Mary. Virginia is a "noble creature," directly compared to "a lilie whit" and "reed a rose" (VI.31–34). This tells us very little, and, as if to underscore this, the Physician merely confirms twice that "excellent was hire beautee" (VI.7, 39). This emphasis on her whiteness and her beauty is illustrative of female virgin martyrs' lives in general. Thus, for example, in the *Second Nun's Prologue,* St. Cecilia is described simply as "faire Cecile the white" (VI.115),[6] and in the earlier *Life of St. Margaret* in Cambridge, Corpus Christi College 303, Margaret is styled "wlitig and fæger," using lexis often associated in medieval texts with Christ's countenance ("naturally beautiful and fair").[7]

---

[6] All references are to the respective *Tales* from Larry D. Benson, gen. ed., *The Riverside Chaucer*, 3rd edn. (Oxford: Oxford University Press, 1987), by fragment and line numbers.

[7] Elaine Treharne, "The Life of St. Margaret," in *Old and Middle*

As with many of Chaucer's other tales, then, in the Physician's choice of hagiography, with this emphasis on Virginia's saintly disposition and countenance, Chaucer appears to be adhering to the conventions of his selected genre. However, all is not as it seems and instead of the usual virgin martyr saint's life, Chaucer's subtle critique of the hagiographic begins to emerge on close examination of the lexis, imagery and historical setting. Notably, the inherent naturalness of the holy saint is deliberately undermined in the depiction of Virginia; indeed, as Patterson has pointed out in relation to the genre of hagiography in the mouth of the Physician, there seems to be significant emphasis in this *Tale* on the counterfeit.[8] In addition to the points raised in Patterson's discussion, this counterfeiting he identifies — a disparity between appearance and reality — also consciously extends to the lengthy opening passage that purports to describe Virginia (VI.4–71). Here, over the course of sixty-seven lines, the Physician tells us very little that is not stock characterization of the saintly female, except that even this two-dimensionalized sequence of attributes is rendered, if not wholly redundant, then at least suspicious by the first twenty-five lines. These focus repetitively on the manufactured artwork of an artisan, not the effusion of beauty one might expect from a divine creation, or, indeed, from Nature herself. Virginia is "formed" and "painted" (VI.12); her creation is compared in a succession of clauses to the work of classical sculptors, smiths, painters and engravers — Pygmalion (who created a statue so beautiful that he fell in love with it and married it when Venus made it human), Apelles (the Greek artist, famed for his life-like paintings), and Zeuxis, another

---

English: An Anthology, c. 890–1450, 3rd edn. (Oxford: Blackwell, 2009), 309–323; and Mary Clayton and Hugh Magennis, ed., *The Old English Lives of St Margaret*, CSASE 9 (Cambridge, Eng.: Cambridge University Press, 1994), 154. This *Life of Margaret* is used as an example of a typical medieval saint's life.

[8] Patterson, *Chaucer and the Subject of History*, 368–369.

Greek painter, who composed a picture of Helen made up of images from other beautiful women. Each of these famous classical artists, then, makes more complex the allusions of Nature to the counterfeiter. This, coupled with Nature's repetition of the creators' skills of forging, beating, engraving and painting strengthens the theme here of a female subject being manufactured, rather than naturally created. Moreover, Nature acting vicariously for "the formere principal" (VI.19) forms and paints "erthely creaturis" (VI.21), reinforcing the persistence of artifice as a major aspect of this long passage.

In making evident the "erthely" as opposed to the heavenly, and the hand-made as opposed to the divinely created, it might be no surprise that Virginia, far from emerging as a perfect exemplum of a saint in human form as virgin martyrs and ultimately all saints are, becomes instead artificial, counterfeit, an ornament, a work of art.[9] In this, and in the repeated emphasis on the manmade, Virginia becomes, in this initial descriptive passage, idol-like, an object to be venerated by those who know no better. And, as will happen to those who break the commandments ("Thou shalt not make to thyself a graven thing, nor the likeness of any thing that is in heaven above, or in the earth beneath, nor of those things that are in the waters under the earth"),[10] the worship of Virginia results in death, both for her and for Apius, the lecherous false judge who lusts after her body.

§ MANIPULATING EXPECTATIONS: TRUE AND FALSE

In spite of being set within a classical, pagan world, Christianity is anachronistically introduced into a *Tale* that, as

---

[9] One might compare, for example, the divinely inspired, innate and post-natal holiness of a saint like Nicholas, who fasted twice a week even as a newborn (Elaine Treharne, ed., *The Old English Life of St Nicholas* [Leeds, U.K.: Leeds Studies in English, 1995]).

[10] Exodus 20:4, *The Holy Bible: Douay-Rheims Version* (Charlotte, NC: St. Benedict Press, 2009).

a consequence, effectively plays with spiritual and practical tenets and *mores*, such as the maidenly preservation of virginity and the commandment to honor one's father and mother. There are numerous pointers to a shared frame of reference between this *Tale* and a traditional *Passio*, like that of St. Margaret's.[11] The textual parallels serve initially to dupe the audience into believing that this *Tale* will unfold with the salvation of the subject saint, even if through that saint's martyrdom. Thus, for example, in admonishing parents and guardians to protect their children and wards, the Physician warns that:

> Under a shepherde softe and necligent
> The wolf hath many a sheep and lamb torent. (VI.101–
> 102)

An unprotected St. Margaret, when approached by her persecutor, the reeve Olibrius, similarly becomes the prey:

> Ac asænd me, leofa Drihten, þinne halga engel to fultume þæt Ic min gewitt and minne wisdom forðhealdan mote, forþon Ic eom gesett betweonen þisum folce swa swa sceap betweonon wulfum, and Ic eam befangan eal swa spearwe on nette, and eall swa fisc on hoce, and eal swa hra mid rape.

> [But send me, dear Lord, your holy angel to help me so that I might hold fast my understanding and my wisdom, because I am set between these people just like a sheep between wolves, and I am entirely caught

---

[11] For versions of the *Life of St. Margaret* circulating in the later Middle Ages, see Katherine Lewis, 'The Lives of St. Margaret of Antioch in Late Medieval England: A Gendered Reading," *Studies in Church History* 34 (1998): 129–142. We do not need to pinpoint a particular *Life* that Chaucer may have known, and I am not suggesting that Chaucer knew the twelfth-century English *Life* used as an example of the genre here.

like a sparrow in a net, and like a fish on a hook, and just as a body with rope.][12]

This metaphor of prey and stalker is as appropriate for Virginia in her plight as it is for Margaret in hers. Margaret is tormented, tortured and executed on Olibrius's commands because she will not give herself physically to him. In the fullest accounts of her *Passio*, there is a significant emphasis, too, on the saint's corporeality, specifically in sharp contrast to the sterility and insensibility of heathen idols and their pagan worshippers. This contrast between the sensate saint and the insensate false god is made obvious in traditional hagiography, but in Chaucer's *Physician's Tale*, the paradoxical integration of antithetical convention in the person of Virginia is, presumably deliberately, perplexing. The 'puzzle' or paradox is that Virginia is saint-like in demeanor and description, yet pagan in background — an apparent Christian (before Christianity existed) and thus the victim of a purposeless death. The narrative elements that we should expect to be true of a saint's life (that the saint is saved, the persecutors damned; the saint taken heavenward, the demon defeated) prove to be false. Yet these hagiographic elements persist; Apius, for instance, becomes possessed by "the feend" that "unto his herte ran / And taught hym sodeynly that he by slyghte / The mayden to his purpose wynne might" (VI.130–132). The demon thus insinuates the idea that Virginia can be Apius' for the taking. Demonic possession is a common phenomenon in saints' lives,[13] where it functions as a mechanism to demonstrate the saint's ability to cure the possessed through exorcism of the devil; as God's grace works through the saint, so the devil's hold of the victim

[12] Treharne, "*The Life of St. Margaret*," 312–313.

[13] Regarding demonic possession, the Lives of St. Giles and Swithun are representative examples. See Peter Brown, *The Cult of the Saints: Its Rise and Function in Latin Christianity* (Chicago: University of Chicago Press, 1981), 106–112.

is lessened. At this point, the medieval audience, listening to the Physician tell his *Tale*, might have felt certain that Virginia would be permitted to demonstrate her saintly *potentia* and cast out this fiend inhabiting Apius. That this does not happen, that she has no power at all, disturbs a motif common in hagiographic narration and unequivocally intimates that God does not work through Virginia, despite her tragic exclamation, "Blissed be God that I shal dye a mayde!" (VI.248). She might bless God, but he surely does not reciprocate. More poignant still are her words to her father, Virginius, when he has declared that he must kill her:

> "Goode father, shal I dye?
> Is there no grace, is there no remedye?" (VI.235–236)

Where a father would commonly protect his daughter, and where God the Father would commonly provide grace and remedy for his chosen, Virginia is abandoned, bereft of paternal care. The complexity of "remedye" here, with a polyvalence that ranges from "legal redress" to "relief from pain and trouble" to "help with a problem" to "deliverance from damnation," is especially pertinent to the pseudo-legal and spiritual dilemma with which Virginia is faced.[14] Of particular note, too, is the quotation provided in the *Middle English Dictionary* from *Ancrene Wisse* (Cambridge, Corpus Christi College, 402), 94/22: "We schulen nu speoken of þe uttre [temptation], 7 teachen þeo þe habbeð hire hu ha mahen wið godes grace ifinde remedie." Here, it is God's grace that will lead to the remedy of avoidance of sin and ultimately, then, salvation. Virginia lacks grace, lacks remedy, and, ultimately, lacks salvation. The Physician's final Christian truth, "Forsaketh synne, er synne yow forsake" (VI.286), underscores the need for his pilgrim audience to seek grace

---

[14] *Middle English Dictionary, s.v.* "remedie," http://quod.lib.umich.edu/m/med/.

and remedy, in a way that was not possible for the heroine of his narrative.

§ MANIPULATING EXPECTATIONS: AUTHORITY AND CHAOS

Throughout the *Physician's Tale*, then, Chaucer undermines the chosen genre of hagiography, problematizing its conventions and usurping the audience's expectations of a saintly reward for saintly behavior. In addition, Chaucer focuses upon the theme of authority within hagiography, or rather, in this *Tale*, the absence of it. Those who are in authority — Apius and Virginius — behave perversely (Patterson's description of Viriginius as "delinquent" seems particularly satisfactory[15]), acting precisely contrary to their prescribed roles as upholder of the law and caretaker of the child. The Physician seeks to emphasize control and authority in his mini-sermon on the duties of governesses and parents (VI.72–104) and in his sequence of potential moral readings (VI.277–286), but as the teller of the *Tale* he resigns control by failing to provide a satisfying denouement. Instead, what the Physician's *Tale* effects is momentary chaos, virtual madness, as the Host

> gan to swere as he were wood;
> "Harrow!" quod he, "by nayles and by blood!
> That was a fals cherl and a fals justice." (VI.287–289)

The Host understands the dominance of the "false" (the counterfeit) in this *Tale*; he apprehends the reprehensibility of the lies of Claudius and Apius, and he knows that for Virginia "Hire beautee was hire death, I dar wel sayn" (VI.297), but the significance that should pertain to a hagiography — the sacrifice of the saint, the fortitude in the face of persecution, the salvation that results from perseverance in God's name — is completely lost in the Physician's telling, effectively

---

[15] Patterson, *Chaucer and the Subject of History*, 389.

destroying the generic signifier. The Host, in a pair of antithetical statements, sums up the paradox:

> This is a pitous tale for to heere.
> But nathelees, passe over; is no fors. (VI.303–304)

The *Tale* is simultaneously pitiful and of no consequence. The phrase "is no fors" is, in itself, easy to dismiss ("it doesn't matter"), and self-reflexively guides the reader to ignore the *Tale* and its rag-bag of morals, but it can be rendered more meaningful if the multivalent potential of "fors" as "value," "authority," and "spiritual strength" are recognized as part of the playfulness here.[16]

The absence of moral and spiritual force in the *Tale* is, arguably, to be expected, if the Physician's own lack of understanding of the Bible is taken into account ("His studie was but litel on the Bible," *Canterbury Tales Prologue*, line 438). He might control life and death for his patients, but he clearly cannot control the spiritual outcome of his patients' lives, and especially so, given his own lack of religious authority. He also cannot control the outcome of his *Tale*, or rescue his female subject from not mattering a jot, despite her saintly piety and virginity. The telling of saints' lives — their narration in church services or when privately read in pursuit of Christian exempla by which to live — should open the way for salvation, and *should* matter. Here, however, the whole function of the hagiography is occluded and its validity (perhaps specifically in the mouth of the ignorant) questioned. The convergence in this *Tale* of the hagiographic topoi littering the narrative with the pagan setting together with the ironic depiction of fatherly protection and legal process creates a response in readers of puzzlement, of a feeling of dissatisfaction.

This dissatisfaction arises from the combination of hagiographic topoi ill employed and the usurpation of generic

---

[16] *Middle English Dictionary*, s.v. "force."

convention. The dismemberment of a Christian saint (Margaret, Agnes, Juliana, Catherine, Cecilia), her decapitation in the pursuit of salvation that is always explicitly assured in the narrative, renders effective the sign of the Saint as a means of demonstrating the efficacy of God's grace. In this *Tale*, the sign of sanctity is itself dismembered, fractured. Semioclasm — the breaking of the sign — occurs elsewhere, and literally, in the *Canterbury Tales*, when the least saint-like of the female pilgrims, the Wife of Bath, deliberately rips three leaves from her husband's Book of Wicked Wives and then makes him burn the book (III.790–791, 815). Here, the literal semioclastic act involves the destruction of the words the Wife finds so offensive. In the *Physician's Tale*, the beheading of an apparently saintly female by her own father, and the text's inability to save her soul, or make of her death any "fors," renders the genre of hagiography that this *Tale* employs redundant. Chaucer's hagioclasm, his breaking of the saintly paradigm, rightly causes consternation and calls into question the genre, its tropes, and its usefulness as a model for the behavior. As so often, then, Chaucer insists on filling the space between text and reader response with questions and reflection, insightfully critiquing the cultural and religious commonplaces of his day and demanding the same critical perception from his audience.

The Light Has Lifted
Trickster Pandare

Bob Valasek

Pandare's role in Chaucer's *Troilus and Criseyde* has been one of much debate among Chaucerian scholars and critics: Is he friend or is he foe, and what is his purpose either way? He is at once friend, foe, and I would argue, the character with whom readers most identify. Readers of *Troilus and Criseyde* realize that they read to discover characters exactly like Pandare; characters whom he or she wishes they could be, and ones whose motives are sprinkled with hints of darkness and mischief. Pandare represents the private thoughts in our minds, the kind we know we cannot, and will not, act upon in the way Pandare has, but which we desire to pursue vicariously. Pandare is a charismatic trickster figure.

The trickster figure is a mythical character found in almost every culture throughout history and is included by Carl Jung among his archetypes.[1] The trickster and its tendencies exist in all of us; the degree to which they surface depends on the individual. Usually a male, tricksters can be identified by many common traits such as stubbornness, chicanery, duplicity, and the ability to evoke laughter. Classic trickster characters range from Prometheus, known as one of the first tricksters, to Uncle Remus's Brer Rabbit.[2] The trickster

---

[1] See Carl G. Jung, *The Structure and Dynamics of the Psyche: The Collected Works of C.G. Jung* (New York: Pantheon, 1970).

[2] See Joel Chandler Harris, *Uncle Remus: His Songs and Sayings* (New York: D. Appleton and Company, 1881).

typically preys on weaker characters and remains confident until the end. The story surrounding the trickster and its result or lesson is often used to satirize the darkest conventions of the culture in which the story takes place. Their mischievous, self-serving actions can often have the trickster backtracking and succumbing to fate or fortune, and through their blunder knowledge can be gained.

Although Pandare is not sinister and is not out to harm Troilus or Criseyde, he embarks on the task of bringing them together not so much for their sake as for his own. He takes pleasure in living vicariously through Troilus while acting as the go-between, the messenger. His stated purpose is dubious at best. The explanation that Pandare is acting purely out of the good of his own heart is entirely too simplistic for this character.

Chaucer creates the setting for *Troilus and Criseyde* during the Trojan War. The war is in full swing, and Troilus, one of Troy's great warriors and son of the King, is discussing his distaste for love. The people of Chaucer's time were all familiar with the war, its stories and its characters. This shows us that from the very start the reader most likely knew this was a tale of inevitable doom.

Book I begins with the narrator telling us of Troilus's "double sorwe" (I.1).[3] Not only does Troilus suffer the pain of being in love, but he is also afflicted by a lover who leaves him for another. The reader, of course, is not aware of this yet. We are introduced to Pandare for the first time in line 548. The narrator tells us that he is Troilus's friend. Pandare is also Criseyde's uncle and her only male relative in all of Troy. As a verb, "pander" means to "minister to the immoral urges or distasteful desires of another, or to gratify a person with such desires," and also to "indulge the tastes, whims, or weaknesses of another."[4] This term's etymology is derived from Pandarus

---

[3] All citations of Chaucer's *Troilus and Criseyde* are from *The Riverside Chaucer*, gen. ed. Larry D. Benson. 3rd edn. (Boston: Houghton Mifflin, 1987), cited by book and line numbers.

[4] *Oxford English Dictionary*, v. "pander."

himself (as a literary character in Latin, Greek, Italian, and English literature) and falls right in line with many of the characteristics of the classic trickster who was previously discussed. We even see this when Pandare asks Troilus, "What unhap may this meene? Han now thus soone Grekes maad yow leene?" (I.552–53). This line precludes two very important points. First, that Pandare is invoking the ruling force of fortune already, and second, that he believes fortune is playing a trick on Troilus. This is not the first time fortune has been referenced in Book I, for the narrator remarks that, "and thus Fortune on lofte and under eft gan hem to whielen bothe aftir hir course, ay whil that thei were wrothe" (I.138–140). Fickle Fortune will eventually lead Troilus to his undoing and thwart Pandare's selfish plan.

Pandare struggles to discover the reason for Troilus's weeping, and finally convinces Troilus to divulge that he has fallen in love with a beautiful woman named Criseyde. Pandare proclaims that this Criseyde is his niece and that he will devote himself to bringing about their union. Pledging his support, Pandare declares, "In this affair, I'll take the strain and stress, and yours be all the joy of my success" (I.1042–1043). We are led to believe in Book I that Pandare sincerely wants to help Troilus and his niece, Criseyde, because he is fond of both of them and would like to see them enjoy each other as he believes they could. Pandare, however, hints towards his selfish motives when he refers to "oure bothe labour shende, I hope of this to maken a good ende" (I.972–973). Pandare has already made this his conquest to undertake, a conquest that will, upon its attainment, be cause for his own happiness by creating a dramatic romantic narrative currently lacking in his own life, and that will require the slippery workings of a skilled trickster.

Book II begins with the first meeting of Pandare and Criseyde. Pandare pays her a visit at her palace. He uses the "I have a secret, but I can't tell you" approach to pique Criseyde's curiosity. He plays on her every emotion, for he knows she is vulnerable. The sign of a successful trickster is his ability to manipulate, and his manipulation can reach its peak when he has the ability to read his subjects well and play off of what he knows. In this case, Pandare knows Criseyde has recently been widowed, and her father has become a traitor in the war, leaving her alone in Troy. Pandare explains to Criseyde that the news he has to tell her is better than news of the war ending, which of course would be the greatest news that Criseyde could ever imagine. After much back and forth, Pandare finally tells Criseyde that it is Troilus who loves her. He follows this news by telling Criseyde,

> that , but ye helpe, it wol his bane be. Lo, here is al!
> What sholde I moore seye? Doth what yow lest to
> make hym lyve or deye. But if ye late hym deyen, I wol
> sterve – have here my trouthe, nece, I nyl nat lyen – al
> sholde I with this knyf my throte kerve." (II.320–325)

Pandare is essentially giving Criseyde an ultimatum: Either she will love Troilus, or she will be responsible for two deaths. He plays her emotions, in this case love and guilt, like a violin, knowing exactly which notes to play at the precise moment, and the ensuing song belongs entirely to him.

We also see Pandare employing fear tactics in Book II. Criseyde's greatest trouble at this time is the war, and she has already made it clear that the war worries her greatly by remarking, "I am of Grekes so fered that I deye" (II.124). Pandare knows this, and makes up a story about Poliphete bringing charges against Criseyde. Her family also fears such a situation, and Pandare is hoping that this fear will force Criseyde to seek protection, the kind that only a soldier such as Troilus could give her.

As was mentioned before, laughter and the ability to make others laugh are two key components in the trickster's repertoire. We certainly see Pandare in this light. Pandare jokes about food when he refuses her invitation to eat with her. He quips, "I have so gret a pyne for love, that everich other day I faste" (II.1165–1166), which plays off of Troilus's inability to eat because he is so lovesick. This causes Criseyde to laugh so hard that she "for laughter wende for to dye"

(II.1169). Pandare jokes to endear himself to others and to break any tension that might be building or already exist, which allows him greater freedom of manipulation and voyeurism, drawing him closer to filling the dramatic narrative void in his life.

The final trickster action worth noting in Book II begins when Pandare invokes the god Mars in line 988. We saw earlier in Book I Troilus aligning himself with Venus, and we now see Pandare aligning himself with Mars, the god of war. Mars is also known for having been caught with Venus by her husband, Vulcan. This can be viewed as a foreshadowing of Criseyde's unfaithfulness. That Pandare should choose an ally such as Mars when trying to start a love affair is rather curious. A god of war has a rightful place on the battlefield and could be appropriate if Troilus were attempting to win Criseyde's heart through a feat of arms, but that is not this case here. Venus, the goddess of beauty and love, is a much more appropriate choice. We can conclude that Pandare's intentions may not be in alignment with Troilus's, and the foreshadowing casts a dark cloud over the potential romance.

Book III brings to light Pandare's barren love life as a possible reason for his trickery. The narrator mentions a few times that Pandare has an object of his affection, but has had no luck in his pursuit. Out of this failure is born a potential explanation for his involvement with Troilus and Criseyde. If he can bring the two of them together, it will be a personal triumph, a way to show the world that he "still has it." A successful union of Troilus and Criseyde as a result of Pandare's deft maneuvering could be just the dramatic narrative void-filling ego-boost that Pandare is seeking, and that, however dark, we all seek in various ways. He stands to gain little else from their courtship. He can prove to himself and Troilus that he knows the ways of women and the ways of love. Troilus's recognition and receipt of the benefits of this would serve to validate Pandare's viability; his ever-important male ego would remain intact. At one point, Troilus even offers to provide one of his sisters for Pandare as a "thank you" compensation for all of his work, granting that he is successful in his quest. He is a very likeable character because the reader gets to walk in Pandare's shoes without suffering the potential consequences. This appealing side of Pandare fits well with the trickster type.

To further the selfish theme that Pandare is cultivating for the reader, Book III also finds Pandare climbing into bed with Criseyde. At this point in the poem, Pandare has begun to associate himself with Troilus and is almost unable to separate himself from Troilus. It is *their* quest, and Criseyde is the object of *their* affection, not simply Troilus's. Both men will suffer if Criseyde rejects love, not just Troilus. This inseparability points to Pandare's vicarious desires, and perhaps also a desire to always be joined to Troilus in some fashion. He has maneuvered his way into this situation by preying on weaknesses and emotions, and he is hoping to regain his swagger once the union is set. Pandare wants more than just a successful relationship between his friend and his niece; he wants the success to fill the void in his own life. Unfortunately for Pandare, he has left fortune out of his equation.

In Book III we also find that Criseyde has become upset upon discovering that Troilus is having some jealous feelings. She interprets his jealousy as distrust, but he tries to spin it as his love goes so deep that he can't help but worry. His whole life would fall to pieces if Criseyde were to be unfaithful. This marks the beginning of the end for Pandare's quest.

Book IV brings us Pandare advising Troilus to take another woman since the situation is beginning to look bleak with Criseyde. This is a shallow suggestion, and serves to further exemplify Pandare's selfish manner. He again refers to Criseyde as "ours" when speaking with Troilus, and advises, much to Troilus's dislike, that Troilus should follow in the steps of Paris and flee with Criseyde regardless of the consequences. This would serve Pandare just fine, for his quest would be complete, even though the lovers may meet uncertain and compromising circumstances. Troilus rejects this idea, electing instead to trust his partner and wait for her promised return.

Book IV also provides three stark instances highlighting Pandare's selfish, rather than selfless, motivation. First, when Pandare visits Troilus after learning of Criseyde has been summoned to the Greek camp, he gazes upon Troilus's sad state and the narrator remarks that this "Seyng his friend in wo, whos hevynesse his herte slough, as thought hym, for destresse" (IV. 363–364). Second, Troilus notes Pandare's love life's troubled past when he say to Pandare, "thou hast has in love ay yet myschaunce and kanst it not out of thyn herte dryve" (IV. 491–492). Lastly, Pandare attempts to steer Troilus away from his own selfless line of thinking by extolling him to "Devyne nat in resound ay so depe ne preciously, but help thiself anon" (IV 589–590). By the end of Book IV, by including these clear markers of selfish intent, Chaucer illuminates the reader's deviant connection to Pandare.

Book V, the final Book, includes the last contact between Troilus and Pandare. Chaucer nearly silences Pandare in the final scene, striking a significant contrast to his normally loquacious and effusive personality. At this point, Troilus's heart has been broken and Pandare is aware of the circumstances. Pandare's failure is actually highlighted by Troilus's broken heart, yet he reader focuses not on Troilus's pain, but instead on Pandare's missed opportunity. Troilus is not upset at Pandare despite his elaborate plan causing Troilus so much pain (double sorrow). Had Troilus been furious, the reader may feel differently toward him and Pandare both. Pandare tells Troilus that he will never forgive Criseyde for what she has done, and we believe Pandare. Criseyde proved through her infidelity that no human being could control fate and fortune, even with the best-laid plans. To count on this union to validate his self-worth was a foolish undertaking by Pandare, but the reader still feels for Pandare rather than Troilus. This misdirected empathy lifts the light for the reader, revealing a darkness in them in a way that few literary characters succeed in revealing.

We learn a lesson from Pandare's error in judgment, just as we do from most trickster tales. The trickster exists to teach us lessons about life and ourselves. We learn from Pandare that there are certain aspects of life that we can control, and many that we cannot. In his case, attempting to control the emotions of others for his own personal satisfaction is his grave error. Pandare lives on though, as most tricksters do. Pandare fails, and like any good trickster, he can be expected to strike again, just as readers will continue to seek characters who mirror the secret tricksters in all of us.

⊙ Suffer the Little Children, or, A Rumination on the Faith of Zombies

Lisa Weston

In modern psychological parlance rumination names a neurotic brooding, a persistent, relentless mental replaying of a bad memory. In a more medieval context rumination is the practice of "chewing over" a well-known and constantly re-read text to achieve insight into the nature of God and the universe. What follows here is, in a way, a cross-temporal rumination or (to alter the alimentary metaphor a little) a worrying of a text of a text that worries me.

The *Prioress's Tale*'s narrative of the Litel Clergeon's death, partial resurrection and second death is a text that I for one have never satisfactorily digested. The story is an (alas) familiar medieval reflex of the blood-libel: a pious young child is murdered by Jews as he walks the ghetto singing a Christian hymn. But the lurid details of this narrative replay themselves, I expect, in many a reader's memory: the slaughtered child hidden in shit; the frantic, weeping mother; the abbot, astounded and confounded by the miraculous discovery of the corpse; the outraged Christian crowd caught up in anti-Semitic rhetoric and bloody vengeance; and especially, at the center of it all, the grotesque body of the Litel Clergeon itself. For it is not, after all, a living seven-year-old boy who sings: it is, rather, his corpse that will not shut up. Nor is that corpse merely moaning or shrieking: that it sings a hymn like *O Alma Redemptoris Mater*, and might (theoretically) sing it forever unless re-murdered, makes the dark grotesquerie of the spectacle of this undead child all the more pervasive. Throat slit, as the Litel Clergeon says, "unto my nekke boon" (VII.649),[1] the child's body serves as an eloquent witness to the power of God, yes, but hardly to anything like the mercy or love proclaimed in the hymn. For that ghastly singing body is stuck, zombie-like, forever on the verge of dying, a victim of violence producing future violence and propagating further victims.

"Zombie-like" is, of course, my early twenty-first century intervention into the late fourteenth-century text. Chaucer's Litel Clergeon is by no means literally one of the shambling, decaying hulks that seem to be our monster-du-jour. Nor indeed even is he quite one of the mindless revenant slaves who, in Afro-Caribbean folklore and early films like Jacques Tournour's 1943 film *I Walked with a Zombie*, horrify us because we might any of us fall victim (as they have) to malicious voodoo — at least if we (like them) venture into an exoticized and atavistic Haiti. Although by no means sundered from their (post)colonial origin, our current zombies are more fully at home in the contemporary (or near future) Anglo-American world. Our zombies — the zombies of films from George A. Romero's seminal 1968 *Night of the Living Dead* through *28 Days Later* (2002) and *Zombieland* (2009), of graphic novels like Robert Kirkman's *The Walking Dead* (begun in 2003) and novels like Max Brodsky's *World War Z* (2006), and even of the Center for Disease Control's online Zombie Apocalypse Survival Guide[2] — have become, too, more the villains than the victims of their stories. Their voracious and mindless appetite turns those they do not completely devour into more of their own mutant species, swelling their legions of decaying flesh on the march. Indeed,

---

[1] All citations of Chaucer's *Prioress's Tale* are from *The Riverside Chaucer*, gen. ed. Larry D. Benson, 3rd edn. (Boston: Houghton Mifflin, 1987), by fragment and line numbers.

[2] See "Preparedness 101: Zombie Apocalypse," *Public Health Matters Blog*, Centers for Disease Control and Prevention, May 16, 2011: http://blogs.cdc.gov/publichealthmatters/2011/05/preparedness-101-zombie-apocalypse/.

in our popular culture they hunger most specifically for brains: they consume, that is, the organ most symbolic of what distinguishes their victims from themselves. The original victim of the outbreak — Zombie Zero, if you will — may be a "pure" victim of a virus either natural or engineered, but any compassion soon fades into fear, or is at the very least complicated by that victim's new role as a threat that must be exterminated. As the protagonist of the 2010 cable series *The Walking Dead* (based on the graphic novel) explains to a crawling torso that is severed (not at all neatly) at the waist, she probably didn't deserve this fate. And he is sorry. But the most charitable thing he can do is to blow her brains out. Lacking any inner life beyond their instinct to consume, our zombies express our anxieties — sometimes about invasions and plagues of various sorts, political as well as biological; sometimes about conformity or mob violence; sometimes about our own mindless consumption and global scarcity of resources. The symbolic resonances are all the more fraught because (especially in each of these last instances) our zombies both are and are not our selves.

The Litel Clergeon is, of course, a zombie only by the most basic definition: one of the living dead, suspended between both life and death, and personhood and thingness, an object of both fear and compassion. And yet, despite the anachronism of my analogy, our modern pop-cultural obsession with creatures neither living not dead, neither fully part of our domestic present nor of some exotic place and time, can inform our reading and rumination of Chaucer's text of a body similarly neither-nor and both human and thing, a body between categories. After all, for many today the Medieval period is itself inherently zombie-like, neither fully foreign nor domesticated, incompletely dead and past. And recent exhibitions like "Treasures of Heaven" (which has traveled between the Cleveland Museum of Art, the Walters

Art Gallery, and the British Museum)[3] witness a modern fascination with the most characteristically medieval form of living death, the "quaint" and "weird" veneration through relics of neither/nor both/and dead saints and martyrs.

More significantly, perhaps, the Litel Clergeon's elective mindlessness and denial of rationality even before his death is as dangerously fraught as that of our contemporary brain-eating Evil Dead, particularly in its ability to infect its world by exemplifying and provoking unthinking violence in the face of troubling uncertainty. As nameless as any Zombie Zero, the anonymous Litel Clergeon shows a devotion not associated with any understood faith *per se* so much as it is an artificially induced instinct. Having been taught by his widowed mother to say his Ave Maria and to venerate the Virgin, he does so to the exclusion of all else, learning the *Alma redemptoris mater* "al by rote" (VII.522), clueless as to what the Latin might mean. But the Litel Clergeon's extreme reverence is a matter only of degree: even the older child who teaches him the song can only tell him that it praises the Virgin and invokes her aid on the day of our death. "I kan namoore expounde in this mateer," he says; "I lerne song. I kan but small grameere" (VII. 535–536). Actively (or passively aggressively) ignoring the very lessons that might help him to understand the words he mindlessly but reverently repeats, and vowing to learn the hymn even though he should be beaten three times an hour for neglecting his studies, the Litel Clergeon is the more completely innocent and his faith is the more perfect because it is willfully and utterly unsullied by understanding.

To the Prioress the Litel Clergeon constitutes both an object of obsession and a model subject. Like the Litel Clergeon she sings her song to the Virgin, performing her "laude" (VII.455, 460) and praising Divine "bountee" (VII.436, 466, 474). Her ability, she demurs or maybe boasts,

---

[3] See, for example, "Treasures of Heaven: Saints, Relics, and Devotion in Medieval Europe," The Walters Art Museum, http://thewalters.org/exhibitions/treasures-of-heaven/.

is no greater than that of a year-old child, a child even younger (and therefore even more innocent of intellectual understanding) than the seven-year-old Clergeon. She aspires to be the saintly child who praises God even "on the brest soukynge." (VII.458) She aspires, that is, to exceed her hero's uncomprehending mindlessness: she aspires to intellectual zombie-nature. She desires, that is, a faith as "pure" as his, unencumbered by the complexities of ontological and ethical uncertainty, and as "innocent," too, as untroubled by the moral responsibilities of thought. The Prioress's inability to achieve that goal creates a dilemma: her willful narrative construction of this ideal faith depends fully on an even more willful choice of emotional over rational behavior — and on the instantiation of the most violent of regimes of control. For the Prioress, that the Litel Clergeon courts violence in his devotion by singing his Marian hymn as he walks through the ghetto only makes him all the more attractive as a hero. In the "logic" of the tale, perfect faith requires and implies perfect (mindless) victimhood.

The Prioress's narration is peppered with effusive and all but ecstatic impositions of interpretation in the service of emotion and instinctive violence. Nowhere is this more apparent than in her repetition of the most lurid details of the child's death: "I seye that in a wardrobe they him threwe," she insists," whereas thise Jewes purgen hire entraille" (VII.573–574). She harangues her villains:

> O cursed folk of Herodes al newe,
> What may youre yvel entente yow availle?
> Mordre wol out! Certeyn, it wol nat faile,
> And namely, ther th'onour of God shal sprede.
> The blood out crieth on youre cursed ded!
> (VII.575–578)

Just as they replicate Herod's ordering of the Massacre of the Innocents, so also must they replicate his ironic failure. If blood cries out, so does, quite literally, the child's bloody body. Her images and her appeal to proverbial wisdom serve to naturalize and make inevitable anti-Semitic violence like that which follows.

Her consequent construction of the child as a virgin martyr represents an incongruous confusion of hagiographic genres:

> O martir sowded to virginitee,
> Now maystow syngen, folwynge evere in oon
> The white Lamb celestial, quod she,
> Of which the grete evaungelist Seint John
> In Pathmos wroot, which seith that they that goon
> Biforn this Lamb and synge a song al newe
> That nevere fleshly women they ne knewe.
> (VII.579–585)

Her vision confuses the meaningful heavenly praise of the Book of Revelations with the meaningless song of the corpse. The lines also, of course, confuse the circumstances of this male child's secret murder with the sexualized judicial torture and public execution of normatively female virgin martyrs.[4] (Interestingly, a number of my students these days make the same cognitive swivel: perhaps because they live in a culture where child abuse by strangers is so often portrayed as child sexual abuse, they do not see this praise of the boy's bodily virginity as entirely out of place. Some even assume child rape in this instance.) The Prioress's further praise of "this gemme of chastite, this emeraude / And eek of martyrdom the ruby bright" (VII.609–610) prefigures the later management of the singing corpse as spectacle ritually contained by procession, mass and (after the child's second death) his burial in a white

---

[4] The earliest exemplars of virgin-martyrdom, girls like Agatha, Agnes and Lucy, were (according to legend) denounced to Roman persecutions of Christianity by thwarted pagan suitors. Roman law did not permit the execution of virgins; before final death the girls are subjected to attempted sexual violation (both Agatha and the twelve-year-old Agnes were dragged to brothels) as well as exposure and gruesome torture (Agatha's breasts are severed and Lucy's beautiful eyes gouged out).

marble tomb. In the Prioress's language the Litel Clergeon is already a relic, holy and unearthly matter, both dead and alive. His now silent body remains on earth a crystallized history of the violence inherent in his tale; his soul soars to the Heavenly Jerusalem envisioned by Saint John, where it shall sing forever.

Despite such valiant rhetorical efforts to decree a happy ending and to contain the tragic miracle (or miraculous tragedy) of the Litel Clergeon's murder and partial resurrection, however, the universe of the *Prioress's Tale* ultimately remains a dark and capricious one, a world as cruel and inscrutable as that of any twenty-first century zombie. It is a world defined by the emoticon pathos of bereft mothers and the schadenfreude of abused and murdered children. More, as much as in the world of any twenty-first century zombie, in the world of the *Prioress' Tale* mindlessness defends against awareness of a cruel and ultimately inhuman universe. In contemporary horror tales that inhumanity may be that of Lovecraftian entities in deep space or of a godless military-corporate complex at home. In the *Prioress' Tale* the inhumanity is exactly that of a God both immanent and distant, whose power is expressed in obscure hierarchies and motivations.

The tale is set in an anonymous town in a far off *Asye* (VII.488) even as it also evokes memory of Little Saint Hugh of Lincoln in the final stanza.[5] This town is ruled by an anony-

---

[5] The body of nine-year-old Hugh was discovered in a well on 29 August 1255, a month after he had disappeared; under torture a local Jew admitted to killing the child, and was subsequently executed. Shortly afterwards, however, ninety other Jews were arrested and charged with involvement in ritual murder; eighteen of them were eventually hanged and their property confiscated by King Henry III. Lincoln Cathedral also profited from the erstwhile martyrdom, as pilgrims began to flock to the child's shrine. The later date and the executions distinguish Hugh from a small group of mostly twelfth century English saints, William of Norwich (d. 1144), Harold of Gloucester (d. 1168) and Robert of Bury (d. 1181), all young boys

mous and apparently absentee lord, whose justice is administered by an equally anonymous provost. The abbot — "an hooly man, as monkes been or eles oghte be," (VII.642–643) a telling ambiguity — pronounces the appropriate prayers over the singing corpse but cannot either explain or adequately contain the miracle and its aftermath. The most he can do is remove the mysterious *greyne* the Virgin had placed on the murdered boy's tongue, and thereby silence the corpse, and then weep and fall prostrate on the ground before the bier.

Beyond these human rulers, the world is subject to cosmological control vested in the ostensibly compassionate Virgin and opposed in an almost Manichaean way by the malicious Sathanas. It is Sathanas, "oure firste foo, the serpent Sathanas" (VII.557), who out of his own inherent malignity incites the Jews to murder the Little Clergeon for his innocent hymn-singing, an act that he rhetorically inflates to a conscious attack on *our laws reverence* (VII.564). The language here ironically replays the primal Fall of Man, with Sathanas both tempter and representative of Law. But the Jews — a vague and (as ever in this tale) anonymous collective — do not act directly upon his urging with either visceral rage or legal outrage. Instead they hire a "homicide" (VII.367), a paid assassin. To the Prioress and the outraged Christian townspeople he may be "this cursed Jew" (VII.570), but although this phrase neatly collapses the agent and his employers, it cannot fully disguise the fact that his motive is money, not faith. Later, although the very existence of a ghetto in this town is underwritten by the Christian lord's "foul usure and lucre of vilenye" (VII.491), when the child's murder is discovered the lord's provost responds to the mob by arresting not just the one killer but (all?) "the Jewes" and sentencing them to be drawn by wild horses and hanged. The specificity of the execution is typical of this narrative's fascination with violence, but in this case it also reveals

---

whose unsolved murders were popularly attributed to Jewish ritual murder.

beneath seemingly simple (if not exactly innocent) emotional motivations a less palatable because more cynically calculating layer of economic self-interest.

It is, perhaps, to deny this political reality that the narrative offers up the Litel Clergeon as the perfect victim. His radical, Edenic innocence is, after all, oblivious to the fallen world of greed and homicide. A child, he cannot (and after his fortunate demise will never) know the adult world of authorities both secular and ecclesiastical, the world in which the Prioress (by reason of her office as much as her maturity) must operate. Unlike her, the child will never have to endure the world of knowledge, and therefore of sin and guilt. Childish innocence, preserved through his willful ignorance, makes him the ultimate martyr. To imitate and sustain this innocence the Prioress's Tale deploys a pervasive and strategic denial. Sathanas and the Virgin, whose maliciousness and compassion are both recognizably (and understandable) human emotions, act within the tale itself. Behind them and allowing the conflict between them to play out, stands an inscrutable God even more effectively absent than the nameless town's absentee lord. Denial of knowledge is the Prioress' response to such a cosmos and such a God, a God who is inaccessible and, ultimately, unmoved by such things as either the child's life or death or non-life. Or even by the purest and most innocent faith. And this last possibility is perhaps what the narrating Prioress takes most pains to deny.

In the face of such fundamental, denied realities, any reassurance about the Litel Clergeon's purity, about his fortunate escape from the perils of adult sexuality, about his martyr's crown, and his merited reception into heaven is futile. None of these "happy endings" can really redeem the horror of the divine revealed in a miracle that prolongs the child's grisly non-life and provokes further tortures and judicial murders. That kind of horrifying miracle finally confounds both emotion and intellect. The singing corpse confuses categories and consequently disrupts all attempts, by emotion or intellect, to discern any sort of essential, ultimate Good.

In a world where corruption is rampant and where death and failure are so inevitable, the tale's apparent anti-intellectualism, skepticism/distrust of authority, and its willful ignorance may represent the only (failed) way of remaining innocent. And that may be what we today find the most tragically recognizable in Chaucer's text. Like the Prioress, we too require the Litel Clergeon's suffering and especially his second death and transformation into an overcoded sign, something we can force to mean what we want (need?) it to mean. We too sometimes aspire to the faith of zombies. In the face of the latest disaster so luridly displayed on the evening news, some traumatized survivor is sure to give witness: "I still hope, because I believe in a benevolent God Who loves us." The otherwise incomprehensible event is thereby given meaning: it offers an opportunity for faith and "proves" the existence of a paradoxically "cruel to be kind" God. But what if that God is too far beyond human emotions like love, too far beyond human labels like "benevolent," to be intelligible? Be careful, *the Prioress's Tale* suggests, when you pray to such a God. Because if you ask for a miracle, a sign from (and of) God, you might just get one.

The Dark is Light Enough
The Layout of the *Tale of Sir Thopas*

Thomas White

Sir Thopas — Chaucer's "rym" (VII.709) that so disappoints the Host — is not generally discussed in terms of dark moments or abyssal themes. In fact, in its wilful and relentless ineptitude, Chaucer's parody of the tail-rhyme romance represents one of the most sustained comic moments in all of the *Tales*, culminating in Harry's uncompromising interruption. However, beneath the surface of Chaucer's parody of the likes of "Ypotas," "Bevys" and "sir Gy" (VII.898–899), the repeated elision of a specific paratextual feature of *Thopas* in both a large proportion of the fifteenth-century manuscripts of the *Tales* as well the vast majority of printed editions points toward the potential inscrutability not only of medieval textual records but also early-modern and modern records as well.[1] This paratextual feature — Chaucer's use and subtle amplification of the traditional tail-rhyme verse layout — forms part of a focus in Fragment VII of the *Tales* on both the resources available to the English poet writing at the close of the fourteenth century and, more generally, the very act of reading and the problematic nature of interpretation itself.

Gerard Genette has examined at length the function of

---

[1] References to Chaucer's *Tale of Sir Thopas* are from *The Riverside Chaucer*, gen. ed. Larry D. Benson, 3rd edn. (Oxford: Oxford University Press, 1988), by fragment and line number.

various types of paratexts, emphasising that whilst they often occupy a problematic interpretative position as to whether they can be said to "belong" to the text, "in any case they surround it and extend it, precisely in order to *present* it, in the usual sense of this verb but also in the strongest sense: to *make present*, to ensure the text's presence in the world.[2] Genette discusses ways in which authors might exploit the "'undefined zone' between the inside and the outside" constituted by the paratext, and it is this impulse that seems central to Chaucer's use of the traditional tail-rhyme layout.[3] But precisely its status as a paratext — as "a zone not only of transition but also of *transaction*" — marks the *Thopas*-layout with a sense of precariousness.[4] In those manuscripts and printed editions in which the layout is not reproduced, it is "outside" of the text in an obviously fundamental way, whilst in many manuscripts this "transaction" takes the form of the layout's reproduction in a partial, reduced or erroneous manner.

However, though there is clearly a general connection between the concept of darkness and the inscrutability or absence of textual-historical records from the medieval period (cf. the "dark ages"), this essay seeks not to lament the absence(s) of this layout as an unrecoverable failure of textual transmission. Instead, I aim to acknowledge both how the *Thopas*-layout can be read as an important part of the form of *Thopas*, as well as the way in which its paratextual status produces numerous examples of the partiality and textual instability that characterises literary production not just in the Middle Ages but also in the early modern and modern periods. That is, the darkness of an imperfect or inscrutable textual record is not necessarily a kind of loss but rather an opening up of a range of interpretive spaces, speculative entry

---

[2] Gerard Genette, *Paratexts: Thresholds of Interpretation,* trans. Jane E. Lewin (Cambridge, Eng.: Cambridge University Press, 1997), 1.

[3] Genette, *Paratexts*, 288.

[4] Genette, *Paratexts*, 2.

points into considerations of the ways manuscripts and books are "caught up by (or lost to) new systems of reference . . . 'forgotten' at times, and at other times 'transformed.'"[5]

In some ways, therefore, the following discussion mirrors the movement of "Chaucers Wordes unto Adam," in which he foregrounds a stable and authoritative "nature" for books as "my making," only to immediately let them go, reminding us that each time they are "wryten newe" any "imaginary order" is "vulnerable to error and susceptible to 'rape.'"[6] It is not just in his "Wordes unto Adam" that Chaucer seems concerned with issues of authorial self-definition and the often disaggregated and distributable nature of intention in the production of literary meaning: in the prologue to *Thopas* itself there is a strange coherence between considerations of a necessarily fragmentary Chaucerian textual record and his self-representation as an "elvyssh" (VII.703) figure frequently caught staring at the ground.

§ "MY MAKING"

The distinctive layout of the tail-rhyme stanza was a development of the relatively common medieval practice of bracketing lines in order to show rhyme scheme: it was employed by Anglo-Norman scribes in manuscripts dating from the close of the twelfth century and was inherited by

---

[5] Alexandra Gillespie, "Books," in *Oxford Twenty-First Century Approaches to Literature: Middle English*, ed. Paul Strohm (Oxford: Oxford University Press, 2009), 91 [86–103]. The following discussion also owes much to D. Vance Smith's critical stance in *The Book of the Incipit: Beginnings in the Fourteenth Century* (Minneapolis: University of Minnesota Press, 2001) and "Medieval *Forma*," in *Reading for Form,* eds. S. J. Wilson and M. Brown (Seattle: University of Washington Press, 2006), 66–79, particularly his emphasis on form not as an "exclusive intellectual formation, resistant to the material, to the deviant, and to difference," but rather as a way of describing "what [a] poem does artefactually" (69).
[6] Gillespie, "Books," 89.

scribes of Middle English tail-rhyme verse.[7] The layout is a diagrammatic representation of the tail-rhyme stanza's common rhyme scheme of *aabccbddbeeb*.[8] The couplets and following tail-line are copied in separate columns, with brackets linking the tail-line to the preceding couplet, with rhyming tail-lines often linked by brackets as well.

The presence of this layout in the Ellesmere, Hengwrt, and Cambridge University Library MS Gg 2.27 and Dd 4.24 copies of *Thopas* suggests that its use is authorial.[9] Furthermore, Chaucer accentuates its potentially confusing effect through the addition of bob-lines that are without precedence in any surviving tail-rhyme romances.[10] These lines require an additional third column and set of brackets, potentially obscuring the correct reading order of the tale even further [see Appendix 1]. Medieval readers would likely have been more familiar with this layout than their modern

---

[7] Rhiannon Purdie has dubbed this layout "graphic tail-rhyme" in "The Implications of Manuscript Layout in Chaucer's *Tale of Sir Thopas*," *Forum for Modern Language Studies* 41 (2005): 263–273. See also Purdie's *Anglicising Romance* (Cambridge: D.S. Brewer, 2008) for a detailed history of the tail-rhyme stanza form, the English tail-rhyme romance, and the origins of the graphic tail-rhyme layout.

[8] Of course, there is often variation from this basic form: *Amis and Amiloun*, *Horn Childe*, *The King of Tars*, and the first forty-five stanzas of the tail-rhyme *Guy of Warwick* all rhyme *aabaabccbddb*. Other tail-rhyme romances, such as *Percyvell of Gales*, *Sir Degrevant* and *The Avowing of King Arthur*, extend the couplets to triplets to produce a sixteen-line stanza. Others, such as *Thopas*, use stanzas of only six lines.

[9] The unique copy of *Sir Ferumbras* in the holograph manuscript Oxford, Bodleian Library Ashmole 33 — dating from around 1380 — is copied in graphic tail-rhyme, further suggesting it was a feature used by authors as well as scribes.

[10] There are texts copied in graphic tail-rhyme that utilise bob-lines, such as the *The Pistel of Susan*, but Chaucer is the first to add them to the tail-rhyme romance. See E.G. Stanley, "The Use of Bob-Lines in Sir Thopas," *Neuphilologische Mitteilungen* 73 (1972): 417–426, for a survey of the use of bob-lines in graphic tail-rhyme texts.

counterparts, but for both the inconvenience of the reading process it demands is undeniable. The layout is obviously part of the tale that is not available to Harry Bailey or the other pilgrims, although for readers it seems to be an element that Chaucer uses to keep them constantly aware of their navigation through the tale, in turn producing a repeated disruption of an imaginative submersion in the tale-telling contest itself, a fundamental violation of the "continuity of the poetic imagination."[11] As such, recapitulation — a recurring thematic trope during the *Tales* — is here manifested at the level of the page itself, as the reader attempts to reassemble the lines into a workable reading order. The sense of the lines gives an idea as to the order in which they should be read, though the vacuity and conventionality of many of the stock phrases of romance that Chaucer uses complicate this process: reading the tale column by column, for example, certainly does not obscure the narrative to any great extent.

This effect is heightened in those stanzas in which Chaucer inserts his additional bob-lines: the diagrammatic layout appears logical enough, but in fact produces numerous reading sequences and the potential for multiple combinations and recombinations of lines.[12] Chaucer's extension of the tail-rhyme romance stanza with the addition of his own anti-climactic bob lines and his placement of the layout in the context of an examination of generic and poetic forms in Fragment VII of the *Tales* seem part of a broader concern with the act of reading itself, as well as an important aspect of

---

[11] Robert M. Jordan, *Chaucer's Poetics and the Modern Reader* (Berkeley: University of California Press, 1987), 17.

[12] Purdie, "Implications," 267. The fourth bob-line stanza (VII.817–826) goes on to exploit the potentially confusing effect of the three preceding stanzas: "Thy mawe" (VII.823) is like the other bob-lines in that it is a two-stress line placed in the third column, but rather than providing an anti-climactic rhyme at the end of the line, it is the object of the following "Shal I percen if I may," producing a subtle syntactic and rhythmic jolt precisely at one of the more disquieting moments of the tale.

Chaucer's "further attempt...to define both the kind of writing that constitutes *The Canterbury Tales* and, more tellingly, the kind of person who wrote it."[13] These issues are revisited in *Melibee* and *The Nun's Priest's Tale*, and in fact throughout his works, as Chaucer asks again and again "Who are my ideal readers? Who are my real readers? How do my readers read? . . . Do my readers invent my authorial intent? Are my readers my own best fictions? What, in fact *is* the act of reading?"[14]

George Edmondson suggests that part of Chaucer's intent in *Thopas* in adopting a form that differs so markedly from his usual poetic voice was to "[preserve] a native literary form by mortifying it: subjecting it to one form of violence, parody, in order to protect it from another, the juridical violence at the heart of natural history."[15] However, literary appropriation looks not only back to the tradition it seeks to question, but also forward to "future readers who have been preshaped by its dynamic presence;"[16] in the junctures of periods of cultural transition, parody offers tools for both deconstruction and reconstruction, criticism and creativity.[17] The tail-rhyme stanza, the uniquely English tail-rhyme romance and the graphic tail-rhyme layout articulate a sense of tradition, and its fallibility, which is clearly central to the parody of *Thopas*. However, these elements are couched in a tale that exploits the fluid, non-systematic medieval conceptions of genre: *Thopas*

---

[13] Lee Patterson, ""What man artow?": Authorial Self-Definition in *The Tale of Sir Thopas* and *The Tale of Melibee*," *Studies in the Age of Chaucer* 11 (1989): 120 [117–75].

[14] Peter W. Travis, *Disseminal Chaucer: Rereading* The Nun's Priest's Tale (Notre Dame: University of Notre Dame Press, 2011), 14.

[15] George Edmondson, "Naked Chaucer," in *The Post-Historical Middle Ages*, eds. Elizabeth Scala and Sylvia Federico (New York: Palgrave McMillan, 2009), 154 [139–160].

[16] Karla Taylor, "Chaucer's Volumes: Toward a New Model of Literary History in the *Canterbury Tales*," *Studies in the Age of Chaucer* 29 (2007): 47 [43–85].

[17] Linda Hutcheon, *The Politics of Postmodernism* (London: Routledge, 1989), 98.

is in fact much more complex than its "drasty" surface initially suggests, including narrative aspects without precedence in the English romance tradition and other subtle modulations of romance tropes and themes.[18] Both in its content and form, therefore, *Thopas* is not simply *a* romance, or a heartless parody thereof, but also "*about* romance, and the roles of author and audience in its telling."[19] As such, the parodic elements of the tale seem intended not simply to mock medieval ways of knowing, but — through a complex play with genre, constant undercutting of expectation and revoking of poetic imaginative continuity — to reveal, and in some senses even to revel in, the problematic nature of interpretation itself.

As Peter Travis writes, "One reason Chaucer's poetry is so patently open to reader-response criticism is that it is highly conscious of itself as linguistic artifice and of its readers' role as conspirators in the art of making fiction."[20] However, by considering the *Thopas*-layout's particular paratextual effect, Travis' observation can be re-embedded in a conception of the form of *Thopas* that is, following Christopher Cannon, "uniquely *comprehensive*," amounting to

---

[18] See Patterson, "What man artow?" 124–35, and Christopher Cannon, "The Spirit of Romance," in *The Grounds of English Literature* (Oxford: Oxford University Press, 2004), 172–209. As John Burrow originally noted, even the incomplete state of *Thopas* in actual fact belies a structural unity: the number of stanzas in each of the three fitts (eighteen, nine, and four and a half) accords with the ratio 4:2:1. In the Middle Ages this ratio, known as the diapason, was the numerical expression of the mathematical proposition thought to govern the universe as a whole (see John Burrow, "*Sir Thopas*: An Agony in Three Fits," *The Review of English Studies* 22.85 [1971]: 54–58).

[19] Melissa Furrow, *Expectations of Romance* (Cambridge: D.S. Brewer, 2009), 36.

[20] Peter Travis, "Affective Criticism," in *Medieval Texts and Contemporary Readers*, eds. Laurie Finke and Martin Shichtman (Ithaca: Cornell University Press, 1987), 205 [201–215].

> [an] insistence that the form of a text not only
> consists of all the structural levels we traditionally
> anatomize when we refer to "literary form" (. . .
> metre, rhyme scheme, or style . . . metaphors or
> patterns of imagery . . . generic affiliations or plot),
> but of the integration of all those levels, *along with*
> *any other aspect of a particular text which may seem*
> *to structure it.*[21]

§ "WRYTEN NEWE"

Whilst Cannon's formalism is useful in considering the
"poetic *activity*"[22] of the *Thopas*-layout in the context of
Fragment VII of the *Tales*, the various incomplete and partial
realisations of the layout suggest a greater sense of the
inseparability of literary meaning and the physicality of the
manuscript page. Each manuscript or printed version of the
text provides additional literary nuance, or at least
information on conditions of literary production rather than
simple context, to the extent that it is perhaps more accurate
to talk of not one form but multiple *forms* of the tale.

In the Delamere manuscript, for example, the scribe
started copying the tale in the two-column layout but quickly
abandoned that in favour of a single column with rhyming
lines still linked by overlapping brackets. Even in this reduced
form the tail-rhyme stanza and its layout clearly caused the
scribe some problems: the third bob-line stanza is bracketed
wrongly, producing an overlapping and confusing sequence of
brackets. The bob-lines "With mace" and "Thy mawe"
(VII.813, 823) are copied to the right of the main column of
text but are misplaced. As such, the recapitulative and
potentially erroneous reading process the manuscript is only
supposed to *stage* becomes a more intrinsic part of its
individual textual materiality. In British Library, Royal MS

---

[21] Cannon, "Form," 178 (italics mine).
[22] Cannon, "Form," 179.

17.d.xv the original scribe copied the first and second fitts of the tale in a single column without brackets. A later scribe then copied the third fitt in the full graphic tail-rhyme layout and also added brackets to the couplets and paraph marks to the end of the *b*-lines in the first and second fitts. The Royal manuscript therefore provides an insight into ways manuscripts can preserve differing levels of interest in paratextual features between scribes, as well as how they approached the works they copied as never entirely finished, even if by accruing additional paratextual information they might disrupt the original design of the manuscript.[23]

In manuscripts such as British Library, Egerton 2863, the layout's meaning is unraveled even further as it is omitted almost entirely: the bob-lines are separated from the preceding line by a *virgula suspensiva*, but the more disjunctive effect of the multiple columns and brackets is elided. The reduced form of the layout in Egerton 2863 is a precursor to the printed editions of the *Tales*. William Caxton, whose deluxe editions were intended primarily for aristocratic patrons, did not reproduce the layout in any of his editions, an editorial decision perhaps based on the perception of popular metrical romances as somewhat unprestigious by the close of the fifteenth century.[24] Wynken de Worde reproduced the layout in his fourth edition of the *Tales* after consulting a now lost manuscript similar to Hengwrt,[25] but Caxton's elision of the

---

[23] Another significant trend in the copying of the tale and its layout is represented by Royal College of Physicians Manuscript 388, in which the scribe retains the two column layout with brackets linking the *a*-lines, but the bob-lines are either omitted or conflated with the preceding line. This is also the case in the heavily edited Cambridge University Library, Ii.3.26, in which the subsumption of the bob-lines into the preceding *b*-lines is but one aspect of an extensive rewriting of the tale.

[24] Purdie, "Implications," 269–270.

[25] See Stephen Partridge, "Wynkyn de Worde's Manuscript Source for the *Canterbury Tales*: Evidence from the Glosses," *The Chaucer Review* 41 (2007): 326–359.

layout was consolidated by later editions that used his *Tales* as their sole exemplar, such as Richard Pynson's 1492 edition. De Worde's remains the only printed edition to reproduce the layout: modern editions of the *Tales* are marked by a reticence to an aspect of the tale that is present in those manuscripts commonly relied upon for their textual authoritativeness, and as Helen Cooper observes, it is this type of treatment that has led modern readers to tend to think of *Thopas* as "a *narrow* poem" when, in fact, its realisation in the Ellesmere, Hengwrt, Gg and Dd manuscripts, amongst others, intimates towards the potential for a somewhat different reading process.[26]

§ "FOR EVERE UPON THE GROUND I SE THEE STARE"

The examples above, though brief, articulate ways medieval texts survive not simply as part of "a rarified history of literature or an intangible history of ideas,"[27] but also as inherently unstable *objects*, "the material result[s] of inevitably imperfect human labour . . . further disordered by time."[28] In Chaucer's canon, his "Wordes unto Adam" is clearly the most explicit examination of the tension between stabilised authorial meaning and the potential for any text to be "myswriten." However, his self description in the *Thopas* prologue stages a disavowal of his own presence that, in its intimations towards simultaneous authorial absence and presence, functions in a strangely similar way to his "Wordes."

Discussions of Chaucer's brief self-description commonly focus on his short stature and bulging "waast." However, in the images of his averted gaze — "Thou lookest as thou woldest fynde an hare, / For evere upon the ground I se thee stare'" Harry tells him (VII.696–697) — and "elvyssh" appearance in

---

[26] Helen Cooper, *Oxford Guides to Chaucer: The Canterbury Tales* (Oxford: Oxford University Press, 1989), 300.

[27] Jessica Brantley, "The Prehistory of the Book," *PMLA* 124.2 (2009): 632 [632–639].

[28] Gillespie, "Books," 87.

the *Thopas* prologue we are presented with a self-representation incongruous to that of the *General Prologue*, where Geoffrey intimates a rather more outgoing personality ("And shortly . . . hadde I spoken with hem everichon / That I was of hir felaweshipe anon" [I.30–32]). Maybe his hidden face is more than just a sudden bout of shyness, though: in medieval thought the head and face were imbued with complex representational values, the face not only signifying the intellect but also regarded, as in the now proverbial saying, as a window to the soul. The expressiveness of gargoyles and other faces in art, sculpture, and the marginalia of books, as well as the large number of reliquaries of hair and facial features, also attest to this symbolic significance,[29] and it therefore seems noteworthy, even strangely disconcerting, that we cannot see Chaucer's.

This sense of a figure not entirely knowable, or at least somehow apart, is accentuated in the second part of Chaucer's self-description as "elvyssh." The *Riverside Chaucer's* gloss of "elvyssh" as "mysterious, not of this world," lacks the sense of terror that figured in many medieval encounters with elves or fairies, who were often portrayed as intent on committing murder or sexual violence of some kind, taking the form of lamiae or incubi.[30] The term was also more expansive in its temporal dimensions: elves, though closely associated with children in medieval thought, are also what some medieval writers referred to as the *longaevi*, the spectre-like "longlivers" who reside both in the air and on Earth; their age indeterminate, they may be generations old, or perhaps even

---

[29] In periods of unrest, statues and sculptures — such as the thirteenth-century *King of Judah*, from Notre-Dame, Paris — were often beheaded in iconoclastic acts that mirrored the fate of those they represented or were associated with. See, for example, "The Face in Medieval Sculpture," The Metropolitan Museum of Art, http://www.metmuseum.org/toah/hd/face/hd_face.htm.

[30] Patterson, "What man artow?" 132.

already dead.[31] Like the "litel clergon" of *The Prioress's Tale* who, though his throat is "kut unto [the] nekke boon," reminds us that "I sholde have dyed, ye, longe tyme agon" (VII.649–651), there is a sense of the Chaucer-pilgrim as somehow out of time, not just mysterious but perhaps more profoundly incomprehensible. He appears at once young and old (or even already dead), part of the tale-telling contest but also strangely separate from it. So whilst it is obviously potentially hazardous to read too much of Chaucer into his pilgrim persona, this self-description seems apt in its placement prior to the *Melibee-Thopas* section: at the moment he is about to tell/write his own tales he provides us with a self-description that seems to intimate towards just how imaginary any contact with an author must be: we cannot look him in the eye, for he will not share our temporal window.[32]

The abyss between stabilised authorial meaning and the inherent *instability* of any discursively formed knowledge clearly produced a certain amount of creative tension for those authors, like Chaucer, who recognised that "litel book[s]" (*Troilus and Criseyde* V.1789) inevitably stand in place of their authors and in doing so are open to having their meaning unraveled or defiled.[33] However, this is an abyss shot through with the light of scribal and editorial responses that represent how any work of literature is necessarily liable to change. As such, whilst I would not elide the potentially destructive force of the type of textual inscrutability suggested by the various

---

[31] C.S. Lewis, *The Discarded Image* (Cambridge, Eng.: Cambridge University Press, 1964), 122.

[32] Chaucer's self-description at this point always invokes, in my mind at least, Michel Foucault's dramatized closing comments to the Introduction of *The Archaeology of Knowledge*, in which he writes of preparing "underground passages . . . in which I can lose myself and appear at last to eyes I will never have to meet again. I am no doubt not the only one who writes in order to have no face. Do not ask who I am and do not ask me to remain the same" (London: Routledge, 2002), 19.

[33] Gillespie, "Books," 87.

forms of the *Thopas*-layout, such examples serve to force us into history, to acknowledge that manuscripts and books never "contain" texts, but rather exist in an uneasy and complex state of reciprocity with them, through which meaning is made, re-made, lost, and found again.

Appendix 1. Diplomatic edition (by the author) of the layout of Chaucer's *Sir Thopas* as it appears in Christ Church College Oxford Library 152 (VII.797–816)

Into his sadel he clamb anoon

And priketh over stile and stone ⟍ An elfe quene for to espie

Til he so longe hath riden and [and] goon ⟍ The contrye of fairye

That he fonde in a pryve woon ⟍ So wilde

Ffor in that contre was ther noon

That to hym durste ride or goon ⟍ Neither wife ne childe

Til that ther cam a great geaunt ⟍ A perilous man of dede

His name was Sir Olyfaunt ⟍ With mace

He seyde childe bi Teramagaunt ⟍ A non I sle thy stede

But if thou prike out of myn haunt

Heere is the quene of Fayerye ⟍ Dwelling in this place

With harpe and pipe and symphonye

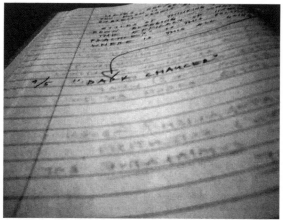

Figure 1. notes toward the beginning of a contributor list
(Eileen Joy's "Hello Kitty" notebook, Brooklyn, 2011)

53962837R00129

Made in the USA
San Bernardino, CA
17 September 2019